Elizabeth II, Queen of Laughs

Stephen Clarke

A book of true anecdotes, quotations and
observations proving that Queen Elizabeth II
is a bit of a comedian.

Author's Note
The author has written a letter
to Buckingham Palace asking the Queen to tell
him her favourite joke, but has yet to receive a
detailed reply. No doubt the Queen knows so
many that she is having trouble deciding.

CONTENTS

Stephen Clarke

INTRODUCTION

She is the only person in Britain permitted to drive a car with no number plates and no driving license. She doesn't even have a passport, so if she's stopped for speeding, the police won't be able to demand ID.

If you meet her in person, you're not supposed to ask her a spontaneous question or even speak until spoken to. You definitely can't touch her, because the only contact permitted by protocol is a quick shake of her hand – if she offers it.

And any breach of this royal fortress of etiquette will be repulsed by what her staff call "the Stare" – a sudden icy glare of total expressionlessness in the Queen's eyes that is said to chill the soul of anyone who meets it.

In short, it's as if the Sex Pistols were right when they famously sang "God save the Queen, she ain't no human being".

Strange, then, that newspapers and magazines so often print photos of the Queen laughing uproariously

Stephen Clarke

at some joke or mishap during a royal family gathering; and that so many people describe one of the happiest laughs they've ever heard when something amuses Elizabeth, as (reportedly) it often does. One of the staff at Sandringham, her English country residence, said that "it is a joyous laugh" and "you can hear her laughter sometimes throughout the house." And the Queen has very big houses.

What's more, she is said to delight in directing her mischievous sense of humour at pompous politicians and dignitaries who forget that they're only human. One of her most famous exploits was getting in the driving seat of a Land Rover and taking the Crown Prince of Saudi Arabia (a country where women were then not allowed to drive) on a high-speed tour of her Scottish estate while he begged her to slow down.

The Queen even directs jokes at herself – to her family, she sometimes refers to herself as "Miss Piggy".

But this apparently incompatible mix of reverence and humour is not the contradiction it seems. When the Queen gives someone "the Stare", it is because they have shown disrespect to her *function*, not to her person. She is reminding the offender that she is not just an elderly lady in a crown or a garish hat – she is the living embodiment of a millennium-old institution, one that plays an integral part in Britain's stability as a democracy. Showing disrespect for her is like throwing a custard pie at a war memorial. It deserves a stare.

One of the Queen's own jokes shows how aware she is of her symbolic role. When she first started doing walkabouts to meet the crowds of spectators during the royal tour of Australia and New Zealand in

1970, she was warned that mixing with the plebs might be dangerous. There were terrorists about, not forgetting republicans and apoliticial maniacs. The Queen shrugged off the warnings, telling her advisors that she had to meet and greet the public because: "I have to be seen to be believed". It's a very neat quote to describe her function, one that a professional wit like Oscar Wilde wouldn't have been ashamed of.

This need to be seen is also the reason why the Queen is known for her uniquely unfashionable outfits, made in colours that seem to have been invented to test the resistance of sunglasses. Despite all the mockery aimed at her dresses and hats by the fashionistas, the Queen carries on wearing them because she knows that she has to be the most visible person at any occasion. It is the opposite of camouflage.

In recent years, as if to defy the mockers, the Queen's colours seem to be getting even more garish. At one of her 90th birthday ceremonies in 2016, she was photographed wearing a green ensemble so bright that digital TV cameras didn't seem to have enough pixels to focus on it.

And it is this keen awareness that she is a woman playing a role that seems to be the key to the Queen's playful sense of humour. She has spent her whole life meeting people who are inwardly or outwardly quaking with nerves in case they embarrass themselves. She, on the other hand, has done it all a thousand times. When you're the coolest person in the room, you're bound to see the funny side of things.

Another factor that shouldn't be forgotten is that the Queen has spent her married life with one of the world's most famous, or infamous, comedians – Prince Philip, who, before his retirement from public life in 2017, kept up a constant stream of "jokes" during state visits and ceremonies that made politically-correct journalists cringe and forced diplomats into apology overdrive. The long royal marriage has never lacked for repartee.

In private, when she can relax, the Queen is known to enjoy teasing even the grandest dignitaries.

Dr Rowan Williams, who was Archbishop of Canterbury from 2002 to 2012, said that this surprised him when he first had meetings with the head of his church.

Dr Williams admitted that he found the Queen "someone who can be ... extremely funny in private – and not everyone appreciates how funny she can be."

This book will try to show exactly how funny that is. It will examine the Queen's sense of humour in all its manifestations, from her first utterances as a child – making fun of an aged Prime Minister, for example – to the more recent videos she has made with Prince Harry and James Bond.

The book will look at quips made at ceremonies, pranks played on everyone from her grandsons to Margaret Thatcher, and jokes aimed squarely at the person who knows the monarch most intimately – Queen Elizabeth II herself.

To correct the Sex Pistols: the Queen, she *is* a human being.

Stephen Clarke

1 A ROYAL FAMILY AFFAIR

In the pidgin English of Papua New Guinea, the
Queen is known as "mama belong big family" – a very
affectionate title. The royals have long referred to
themselves jokingly as "the family firm", as if they
were a long-established fish shop. The late Princess
Diana shortened the name – she dubbed them "the
Firm", apparently a reference to the secretive, Mafia-
embroiled company in the 1993 film of the same name
starring Tom Cruise (who, coincidentally, is about the
same height as the Queen – five foot four, or 162.5
centimetres).

In fact, Diana's description was pretty appropriate
because, like the Mafia, the royals form a tightly-knit
clan who collectively demand that all incomers, either
by marriage or birth, obey their rules. After all, their
whole existence depends on preserving family
traditions. If any generation goes off the rails, the
monarchy could be finished. And what would a former
queen and the princes and princesses do all day if they

weren't invited to unveil statues, launch ships and wear silly hats?

As the most senior members of the family in both rank and age, the Queen and Prince Philip are at the heart of this culture of strictness, and make their disapproval very clear if anyone tries to rock the boat. And the training starts young. Prince William once said as much: "I learned from growing up, you don't mess with your grandmother." He has also said that he has been trained so that he is "open for people saying I'm wrong because most of the time I am." Not something that you'd expect an heir to the throne to admit.

But for all their strictness, the royals do seem to be a supportive family. Even at the height of Princess Diana's crisis, she was getting letters from her father-in-law Prince Philip giving her paternal advice on how to cope with excessive celebrity and marriage to an unfaithful prince.

It's an atmosphere of closeness that seems to have its roots in the Queen's own childhood. She wasn't born to be monarch – her father, then known as Prince Albert, was second in line to the throne after his elder brother, Edward, and at first Elizabeth and her sister Margaret lived a relaxed life of privilege in a tight family unit of four.

For the first ten years of her life, Elizabeth's father was just a shy young man with little to do except fulfil minor royal duties and play with his children. His eldest daughter, Elizabeth, who was born on 21 April 1926, was known to everyone as "Lilibet", a nickname she got when she began to talk and couldn't pronounce her own name.

Not much was expected of Lilibet, either – she didn't even have to study much history as a child, because as a member of the secondary royal line, it was thought that she had no need of historical awareness.

Then in 1936 King Edward VIII abdicated, forcing Elizabeth's father to change his name from Prince Albert to King George VI and put on the crown. With this new responsibility, everything in the household suddenly changed – except the sense of humour that had reigned in the family ever since Elizabeth was born.

Young Princess Lilibet

Some anecdotes from her early life ...

As a very young girl, Elizabeth was a constant source of family amusement. Her grandmother, Queen Mary, the wife of King George V, used to greet her by saying, "Any good new jokes today, Lilibet? You must tell me the latest."

Elizabeth's grandfather, King George V, who is generally remembered as a grumpy, austere figure, used to play with the young Princess in her nursery, he on all fours pretending to be a horse, she leading him around the nursery by his beard.

When Elizabeth was three, her nanny tried to explain why she had to curtsey to her grandfather – all women and girls were obliged to show reverence towards the King. Next time Elizabeth saw George V, she curtseyed, but with her back turned to the monarch – a slightly different gesture.

Once Elizabeth knew that her grandfather was the King, she nicknamed him "Grandpapa England". (Incidentally, many royal toddlers seem to have problems understanding that their older relatives are high-ranking people. The first time the young Prince Harry was told that the Queen was coming to see him, he asked, "Who's the Queen?").

As a very young girl, Elizabeth liked to pretend to be a horse. If someone spoke to her and got no response, she would explain: "I couldn't answer you as a pony."

Elizabeth and her parents used to go to the country for hunting trips. During one of these, they were visited by an earl who lived in a nearby stately home. He arrived on horseback, to be met by the young Princess Elizabeth. "Do please come in," she told him, "but you'd better leave your horse outside."

When she was seven, Elizabeth met the Prime Minister, Ramsay MacDonald, a distinguished old statesman of almost 70. "I often see your picture in the papers," the young Princess said. Ramsay smiled. "Yes, the other day I saw you leading a flock of geese," she added. (She might have been referring to a procession of politicians in their long tail coats.)

It wasn't the first time MacDonald had come off worse in a royal exchange. In 1931 he went to George V and offered his resignation, saying that the economic situation was too bad for him to go on. The King refused, saying: "You've got us into this bloody position; get us bloody well out of it." (Something that the Queen clearly *didn't* say to David Cameron after the 2016 Brexit referendum.)

When Elizabeth was young, her family would often make home movies, with various members of the family singing, dancing and pulling faces. However, this capacity for playing up to the camera backfired when some royal home movies were leaked to the British press in 2015.

A short segment of silent film, less than twenty seconds long, showed Elizabeth and her mother laughing and apparently doing a Nazi salute. The film was shot in 1933 or 1934, and inspired the *Sun* newspaper to create one of its trademark punning headlines: "*Their Royal Heilnesses*".

Some anti-monarchists alleged that the salutes were proof of the royal family's Nazi sympathies before the war. After all, Elizabeth's uncle, King Edward VIII, actually visited Hitler in Munich in 1937, and the Nazis had planned to use him as a puppet king of England if they invaded Britain. But most commentators agreed that the home movie simply showed Elizabeth's willingness to joke around for the camera. In the film, when not saluting, Princesses Elizabeth and Margaret are just leaping up and down and giggling, as little girls do. She and her mother were almost certainly making fun of the Nazis' ridiculous stiff salutes.

And it should be mentioned that someone else was encouraging them to make the salute, and showing them exactly how it was done – Edward.

In December 1936, when Edward VIII abdicated and responsibility was thrust on Elizabeth's father, the new King George VI, life suddenly got serious. Rather than being overjoyed by this sudden ascension, father, mother and the two girls were deeply depressed by the loss of their carefree existence. Princess Margaret, then six, told her elder sister Elizabeth: "Does that mean you're going to be Queen? Poor you."

During World War Two, the royal family famously refused to take refuge in Canada, although they were encouraged to leave England for their own safety. The only precaution taken was to send Princesses Elizabeth and Margaret out to Windsor Castle rather than have them stay in London while the Nazi bombs rained down on the city.

On 13 October 1940, aged 14, Elizabeth gave her first-ever radio broadcast on the BBC, a morale-boosting talk aimed at the many British children who had been evacuated out of their city homes.

Elizabeth's posh accent sounds almost comic today (she pronounced "often" as "orfen" and "and" as "end") but when she called her sister to the microphone to say goodbye, Elizabeth's "Come on, Margaret!" was such a hit that children all over the country adopted it as a catchphrase.

During the war, Elizabeth was a keen participant in royal pantomimes at Windsor Castle, dressing up, singing, tap-dancing and acting – the perfect training for a life of public performances. The audiences were often large crowds of several hundred local people and soldiers, and the shows were almost professionally put together, with long rehearsals and elaborate costumes – in 1941, the teenaged Elizabeth donned a turban and fetchingly tight shorts to play the Prince in *Cinderella*.

The royal performances took on a more serious purpose as the war went on – in 1943 the royals put on a pantomime for three nights and sold tickets to raise money for wool to make soldiers' socks.

The future Queen got excellent training from her parents in the importance of a stiff upper lip during wartime. On one occasion, her father, King George VI, was visited at Buckingham Palace by Wilhelmina, the exiled Queen of the Netherlands. She asked George what would happen if Nazi parachutists suddenly began landing in the palace gardens. "I'll show you," the King told her, and appeared to press a hidden alarm button. Nothing happened. There was no alarm bell.

The royal sense of humour survived right thorough the war. In February 1945, Elizabeth joined the Women's Auxiliary Territorial Service as Second Subaltern number 230873, and put on a uniform, as did many women of her age. This was a great publicity coup, and the Princess was filmed working on the engine of a Red Cross lorry while her parents, King George VI and his wife (the then Queen Elizabeth), visited the training centre. When the royal parents returned to the lorry after inspecting the rest of the base, the King asked his daughter: "Haven't you got it mended yet?" He then revealed that he had sabotaged the engine by removing the distributor.

Near the end of the war, the King, Queen and Princesses Elizabeth and Margaret were having tea on a terrace at Windsor Castle when they heard General Eisenhower and his staff talking below them. The King had forgotten that the Americans were coming for a tour of the castle, and said that it wouldn't look good if the royal family were spotted blithely having tea without inviting their VIP guests. The royals duly hid under the tea table, giggling until the Americans were out of sight.

On 8 May 1945, the day the Nazis finally surrendered, Elizabeth appeared on the balcony of Buckingham Palace with her parents and Winston Churchill to greet the cheering crowds. But this wasn't enough for the 18-year-old princess, who decided to go out and join in the celebrations.

In her Women's Auxiliary uniform, Elizabeth went out with her sister Margaret, their cousin Margaret Rhodes and a dozen or so male and female friends, many of them also in uniform. To disguise herself, Elizabeth wanted to pull her cap low down over her forehead, but one of the men objected that uniforms must always be correctly worn, even off duty.

Princess Elizabeth danced in the streets with the carousing crowds, and even joined the seething masses outside Buckingham Palace, cheering the King and Queen when they returned to the balcony. It was what Elizabeth's cousin Margaret Rhodes called "a Cinderella moment in reverse." Later, the exhilarated princess wrote in her diary: "Trafalgar Square, Piccadilly, Pall Mall, walked simply miles. Saw parents on balcony at 12.30am – ate, partied, bed 3am!"

She escaped from vigilance for a second time on 14 August 1945, the day of the Japanese surrender, doing a conga and returning home at 2am.

By the end of the war, Princess Elizabeth knew who she wanted to marry – a tall, glamorous man who had been writing her letters ever since they first met when she was 13 and he 18. Despite serving in the British Navy, Philip was a Greek prince, and some factions of the royal family were not in favour of this union with a foreigner, especially as the Princess was still so young. To avoid opposition, in her room Elizabeth displayed a photograph of Philip sporting a thick beard, and told staff: "I defy anyone to recognize who that is!"

The young couple had to wait to get engaged until Elizabeth was 21, and they finally married on 20 November 1947. Philip must have realized what he was getting into when he signed the marriage certificate. On the document, Elizabeth's father's profession was given as: "HM King George VI of the United Kingdom of Great Britain and Ireland and of the British Dominions across the Seas; Defender of the Faith." Philip knew that one day his wife's job title would be just as long.

The wedding celebrations were boisterous and humorous. King George VI led a conga line through the corridors of Buckingham Palace, and the menu at the wedding lunch contained jokey items. The first course was *filet de sôle Mountbatten* (as this was Philip's family name, it was presumably a piece of fish as long and pale as the young Prince) and the dessert *bombe glacée Princess Elizabeth*, which sounds like an unfortunate French pun about a chilly sex-bomb, but was in fact a dish containing deliciously naughty out-of-season strawberries.

The honeymoon was not exactly glamorous – the young couple spent a week at the Mountbatten home in Hampshire, then two in the frozen hills of the Balmoral estate, the royal residence in Scotland. There, Elizabeth wrote to her cousin Margaret Rhodes that she went out hunting deer, feeling like "a female Russian commando leader followed by her faithful cutthroats". A less military man than Philip might have begun to worry about what he'd let himself in for ...

A(nother) German Enters the Family

Exactly as the husband of a queen should be, Prince Philip is his wife's cousin. (Well, a third cousin, to be exact, because his mother was a great-grandchild of Queen Victoria.)

And in the best traditions of the British royal family, Philip is basically German. His mother's parents were called Battenberg and Hesse, and she married a Greek prince, but his father was a member of the Schleswig-Holstein-Sonderburg-Glücksburg family.

This historic German-ness was understandably a problem when Philip was courting Princess Elizabeth during World War Two, and he was obliged to give up his foreign nationality (or nationalities) and become

British, calling himself Mountbatten, an anglicization of the old Battenberg title. Even after the wedding, Philip was sometimes snubbed by old-school members of the royal court, and began referring to himself as the "refugee husband".

The Germans are not usually known for their sense of humour, but to Elizabeth's father, King George VI, jocularity was a necessary requisite for his daughter's future consort. George VI told his mother, Queen Mary, that he approved of Philip because he was "intelligent" and "has a good sense of humour." And right from the start, Philip seems to have brought a certain robust jokiness to the marriage …

On their tour of Canada in 1950, Philip was seen chasing Elizabeth along the corridor of a train, baring a set of joke teeth.

In 1954, Philip commissioned a custom sports car for himself, an open-top Aston Martin (there were no calls for royal austerity in those days). He had it fitted with a telephone, from which he would make frequent spoof phone calls to the Queen, disguising his voice. He also had an extra rear-view mirror fitted to the car, telling everyone that it was so that "my wife can adjust her hat".

A characteristic Philip vehicle-related saying is: "When a man opens a car door for his wife, it's either a new car or a new wife."

Philip has always been a big car fan. He even bought himself a real London taxi and used to drive around the city pretending to be a cabbie, with his detective in the back seat as passenger.

Once, a friend of Philip's met Elizabeth for the first time and said, "I never realized what lovely skin she has." Philip replied, "Yes, she's like that all over."

One should not believe everything one sees in highly fictionalized TV drama series, but it is true that the royal marriage hasn't always been a serene one. When the Queen and Philip want on a post-coronation tour of Australia in March 1954, cameramen filming the royal chalet at O'Shannassy Reservoir in Victoria were shocked when the door of the chalet suddenly opened, and Philip shot out, followed by a flying shoe and then the Queen, who was shouting at him to come back and take his punishment.

The whole scene was filmed, but the cameramen immediately erased the footage. The Queen later came out and offered to be filmed, saying, "I'm sorry for that little interlude, but, as you know, it happens in every marriage. Now, what would you like me to do?"

In 1957 Philip went on a tour of the Commonwealth without the Queen. Film and photos of him on his travels showed that he obviously hadn't taken a razor with him, either. When he returned home, hairy-faced, the Queen greeted him wearing a false beard.

In 1966, on their ninth wedding anniversary, Philip was away on a state visit, but sent the Queen a card depicting two iguanas apparently embracing. Not exactly flattering, but quite prophetic, because with advanced age, Philip has since taken on a slightly iguana-like appearance.

When he was a young man, Philip was strikingly handsome, and there were rumours that as a sailor, he had a woman in every port. This would have been pretty impractical given that he visited so many of these ports on the royal yacht, alongside the Queen, but he did go on long solo tours when they were first married, and naturally wherever he went, he attracted the attention of the local ladies. Even though no proof of adultery has ever been produced, the rumours always infuriated Philip, who once said: "The way the press related it, I had affairs with all these women. I might as well have bloody enjoyed it."

Early in their marriage, the Queen and Prince Philip were on a ship crossing from the Canadian mainland to Vancouver Island. The weather was bad, and as a tray of cakes was brought into their state room, the boat lurched and the cakes fell on the floor. Philip quickly got down on his hands and knees and collected up a plateful. He told the Queen: "I've got mine – yours are down there."

The Queen got her revenge in 1976, when the royal couple sailed the Atlantic to visit the USA. One evening, the royal yacht *Britannia* hit heavy seas, and surprisingly, the ex-naval officer Philip suffered terrible sea-sickness, unlike the Queen who was completely spared. Some of their staff were feeling very nauseous too, and were unable to face dinner. Next day, the

Queen said, "I have never seen so many grey and grim faces around a dinner table." She added: "Philip was not well ... I'm glad to say."

When the Queen was first married, she often used to begin speeches saying "my husband and I". In her posh accent, this came out as "may husband end ay", and was imitated by countless comedians. The Queen wisely stopped using the phrase.

But in 1972, at the couple's 25th wedding anniversary celebrations, she joked: "I think everybody really will concede that on this of all days, I should begin my speech with the words 'my husband and I' ".

A Short History of "Dontopedalogy"

In 2017, Philip announced that he was retiring from public appearances. In certain quarters, the reaction must have been a deafening sigh of relief. He summed up the reason very well himself. In 1956, he told an audience that: "It is my invariable custom to say something flattering to begin with so that I shall be excused if by any chance I put my foot in it later on." In 1960, he gave a name to this custom during a speech to Britain's General Dental Council, in which he announced that he had invented a new discipline for them to study: "Dontopedalogy is the science of opening your mouth and putting your foot in it, a science which I have practised for a good many years."

Philip has also admitted that, from the start of his career as a royal consort, his philosophy was "safer not to be too popular. You can't fall too far." His critics would say that some of his attempts at humour fell completely flat. Because apart from being the Queen's husband, what Philip has been most famous for throughout his life is his tendency to commit verbal faux pas. Whenever he was about to appear in public, the royal PR department probably opened up a new Word file beginning, "Prince Philip clearly meant no offence towards ... [FILL IN BLANK] when he said ... [FILL IN BLANK]. What he actually meant was ... [THINK UP CREDIBLE EXCUSE]."

It was not entirely Philip's fault. He seems to have caught his straight-talking habit from his mother, Alice. She once asked one of the Queen's private secretaries to repeat a question. As soon as she had understood, she said, "Oh, I thought you were saying something interesting.

But Philip made the domain of verbal gaffes his own. When in her 2017 Christmas speech, the Queen paid tribute to her husband's "unique sense of humour", she was just being polite. Because, as well as being the British royal family's oldest ever male, Philip is probably the oldest man in Britain whose dubious jokes regularly get on to TV and into the press.

And anyone who thinks that it's all accidental, that he's just an old fool talking nonsense without realizing it, should remember his speech about dontopedalogy. Philip is fully aware that if he really wanted to avoid offence, he could just keep his mouth shut. The inevitable conclusion is that his jokes are all deliberate. In short, the Queen's husband is probably the longest-running comedy act in British history.

On the other hand, his tendency to come out with what are perceived as offensive jokes is probably less deliberate. Despite his mixed origins, Philip is, to all extents and purposes, a typical old Englishman of his generation, prone to making apparently racist and sexist comments. In the 1940s and 50s, his brand of politically incorrect repartee would have been thought totally acceptable. In fact, the only real problem with Philip's jokes is that his sense of humour is as old as he is.

And apart from a few unfortunate exceptions, even the butts of Philip's jokes during his public appearances probably admit that they were usually a well-intentioned attempt to inject a bit of levity into what could otherwise have been a nervous, pompous encounter with royalty. Protocol dictates that people meeting members of the royal family are not meant to speak until they're spoken to, so he would get in there first with a "humorous" ice-breaker.

Sometimes this was harmless jollity: while sitting next to the Queen in a carriage or limousine, arriving at an event, he might choose a random person in the crowd and wave directly at them, purely for the fun of it. At other times, he was very self-deprecating. He once said of his lifetime of visiting universities and laboratories: "My only claim to fame is that I'm the most experienced visitor of technological facilities. I've been doing it professionally for forty years. I can claim to have patted the first microchip on the head."

He has also joked about his inferior position compared to his wife. On one occasion, when he was introduced to an Australian couple, the husband explained that his wife was a doctor, "much more important than me." Philip replied: "Ah yes, we have that trouble in our family too."

Perhaps with his jokes, Prince Philip has just been

trying to show the world that the British royal family is human. All too human, in fact ...

Here is a selection of his politically incorrect, brutally frank, but (usually) well-meaning comments.

First, some mild racism ...

In 1963, while viewing an exhibition of "primitive" Ethiopian art, Philip said: "It looks like the kind of thing my daughter would bring back from her school art lessons."

Once when in Quebec, he annoyed the locals by announcing that he didn't like their accent when they spoke French: "Can't understand a word they say. They slur all their words." (Amusingly, a lot of Parisians would agree with him.)

He also quipped that Canada had turned out to be "a good investment" for Britain. Not exactly how a major Commonwealth nation likes to think of itself, and the Canadian media were suitably enraged.

After accepting a gift from a Kenyan woman in 1984, Philip thanked her, then spoilt the effect by asking: "You are a woman, aren't you?"

While on a visit to China in 1986, Philip met a group of young Brits studying there and told them: "If you stay here much longer you'll all be slitty–eyed."

In 1994 he asked a Cayman Islander: "Aren't most of you descended from pirates?"

When a man in Oban, Scotland, told Philip that he was a driving instructor, Philip asked him: "How do you keep the natives off the booze long enough to get them through the test?"

"And what exotic part of the world do you come from?" Philip once asked Lord Taylor of Warwick, whose parents are Jamaican. Taylor replied: "Birmingham."

"People think there's a rigid class system here," Philip once told an audience in England, "but dukes have been known to marry chorus girls. Some have even married Americans."

In 2002, after being served a luxurious breakfast of bacon, eggs, smoked salmon, kedgeree, croissants and *pain au chocolat* – a gourmet menu invented by French chef Regis Crépy – Philip announced: "The French don't know how to cook breakfast."

He did even things up, though. Philip once told a gathering of British women: "British women can't cook."

Visiting a Bangladeshi youth club in England in 2002, Philip joked with the members: "So who's on drugs here? ... *He* looks as if he's on drugs," he said pointing to a perfectly innocent 14-year-old boy.

Visiting the Aboriginal Cultural Park in Queensland in 2002, Philip asked Aboriginal leader William Brin: "Do you still throw spears at each other?"

In 2009, Philip was introduced to an all-black dance troupe and inquired: "Are you all one family?"

A more general lack of political correctness …

During the economic downturn in the early 1980s, Philip's philosophy was simple: "Everybody was saying we must have more leisure. Now they're complaining they're unemployed. People don't seem to make up their minds what they want."

In 1988, Philip pronounced, rather worryingly for the Queen: "I don't think a prostitute is more moral than a wife, but they are doing the same thing." (In fairness, he was attempting to draw a philosophical parallel between hunting and eating meat.)

At a Buckingham Palace drinks party in 2000, Philip espied a group of female Labour MPs and said: "Ah, so this is the feminist corner."

During a visit to Nigeria in 2003, Philip asked some women what they did. They replied that they empowered people. Philip answered, "Empower? That doesn't sound like English to me."

At a World Wildlife Fund meeting in 1993, Philip asked fashion writer Serena French: "You're not wearing mink knickers, are you?"

Knickers seems to be one of Philip's favourite words, because in 2010 he was discussing tartan fabrics with Annabel Goldie, the leader of the Scottish Conservatives, when he commented: "That's a nice tie ... Do you have any knickers in that material?"

In 2015, Philip asked some women at the Chadwell Heath Community Centre in East London "who they sponge off". Some commentators reacted furiously, reminding people that the royals have traditionally been the nation's biggest spongers. But in fact, it was simply one of Philip's attempts at a pun, because the women had just presented the Queen with a sponge cake.

Some painful insensitivity …

When Philip and the Queen were introduced to a young man called Stephen Menary, who had been partially blinded by an IRA bomb, the Queen asked how much he could still see, and Philip joked: "Not a lot, judging by the tie he's wearing".

Visiting Cardiff, Philip told children from the British Deaf Association, who were standing next to a Caribbean steel band: "If you're near here, no wonder you're deaf".

In 1969, Philip asked singer Tom Jones: "What do you gargle with, pebbles?"

Once, when waiting for guests to be seated at a dinner, Philip exclaimed: "Bugger the table plan, give me my dinner!"

Similarly, at a photo shoot with army veterans, he was filmed telling a photographer who was trying to re-arrange the group: "Just take the fucking photo." (The army men all laughed.)

While visiting the Caribbean in 1966, Philip told the matron of a hospital: "You have mosquitoes. We have the press." (Most people would concede that malaria is a more dangerous affliction than prying paparazzi.)

In Ottawa, Canada, in 1969, Philip told an audience: "We don't come here for our health. We can think of better ways of enjoying ourselves."

In 1997, when meeting then German Chancellor Helmut Kohl, Philip greeted him incorrectly as "Reichskanzler", a title last used by Hitler.

In 2006, while trying to explain the continuing need for his Duke of Edinburgh Awards scheme, a youth programme which encourages physical exercise and autonomy, Philip commented: "Young people are the same as they always were. They are just as ignorant."

Another slightly worrying quote for the Queen. In 1992, asked about the course of his life since his wife became monarch, Philip replied: "I'd much rather have stayed in the Navy, frankly."

However, sometimes it has to be said that Philip's insensitive remarks have been perfectly in tune with public feeling, and the Brits have felt that he was just saying it like it is ...

In 1967, when the Communist regime was still very much in power in the Soviet Union, Philip was asked whether he would like to visit the country. He replied: "I would like to go to Russia very much, although the bastards murdered half my family." (Philip is related on his mother's side to the Russian imperial family.)

In 1999, Philip was introduced to three employees of a Scottish fish farm, and told them: "Oh! You're the people ruining the rivers and the environment."

He showed some more of his environmental sensitivity in 2011 when he told the managing director of a wind-farm company that wind turbines were "an absolute disgrace" and "absolutely useless". Many residents of the British countryside would agree.

At the opening of the British Council offices in Nigeria in 2003, Philip listened to a speech about the Council's aims and objectives, and then commented loudly: "That speech contained more jargon per square inch than any I've heard for a long time."

When meeting a 13-year-old boy called Andrew Adams who said he wanted to be an astronaut, Philip gave some advice: "You could do with losing a little bit of weight."

Once, on getting off a plane, Philip was politely asked by a local: "How was your flight?" He retorted: "Have you ever flown in a plane? ... Well it was a lot like that."

In 2000, at the opening ceremony for a new British Embassy building in Berlin that had cost £18 million, Philip remarked: "It's a vast waste of space."

At an official dinner in Rome, when presented with a list of the best Italian wines, Philip told a waiter: "Get me a beer. I don't care what kind it is, just get me a beer!" A true Englishman (with German blood).

Too Much Information

At the end of the 1960s, an attempt by the Queen to give an insight into royal family life went badly wrong. This was a time when Britain's class system was in upheaval. The Beatles had turned the country on its head, creating a new world in which pop musicians could be at the pinnacle of society, and where a Liverpool accent was more desirable than an Oxford drawl.

It was probably this sense of social renewal that convinced the Queen to make a fly-on-the-wall documentary about her personal life, with television cameras observing the royal family at home – conversations at the breakfast table, Prince Philip cooking sausages for a barbecue, the children squabbling, the Queen buying ice cream in a shop.

When *The Royal Family* was shown in 1969, 75% of the British population turned on their TVs to watch. And were shocked. As one commentator said, it was the first time that anyone had seen the royals talking to each other rather than making small talk at a function or giving a speech, so it was reassuring to hear them having ordinary conversations. But the main feeling among the viewing public seems to have been discomfort. The royals came across as pleasant enough people, laughing a lot and enjoying normal things like campfire sausages, but their upper-class accents were painfully alien. And what kind of mother wears a pearl necklace to a family picnic?

One of the film's producers, the legendary broadcaster David Attenborough (now more famous for his documentaries about slightly different forms of wildlife) explained the fundamental problem with the film, likening the monarchy to the mystique surrounding a tribal chief's hut: "If any member of the tribe ever sees inside the hut, then the whole system of the tribal chiefdom is damaged and the tribe eventually disintegrates."

The Queen duly decided that the documentary should never be shown again, and it disappeared into the royal archives. The only footage that has resurfaced (legally, anyway) is a compilation of short scenes for an exhibition marking the Queen's Diamond Jubilee in 2012.

This royal act of censorship is regrettable if only because during the film, the Queen apparently told some funny stories – one about a dignitary falling over in front of Queen Victoria, and a surreal anecdote about an occasion when she expected to be introduced to a politician, but ended up meeting a gorilla. One day, perhaps, all will be revealed … again.

The Queen and her children

Princess Anne and Princes Charles, Andrew and Edward have always enjoyed lives of great luxury, and will never have to go online to apply for unemployment benefit or a council house, so no one is going to pity them. But their lives haven't always been easy. Like their mother, they have been in the public eye ever since they were born, in an age where the media have become increasingly prurient and decreasingly reverential towards royalty.

Charles, Anne, Andrew and Edward have all had their love lives picked over by the predatory press. And only Charles has been groomed for succession – the others have often been left to their own devices. This probably explains why Elizabeth's children have occasionally been the butt of jokes ...

Princess Anne was a member of Britain's equestrian team at the 1975 European Championships, and won both team and individual silver medals. But these achievements only attracted jibes about being too "horsey". Her father Prince Philip joined in, saying of her in 1970: "If it doesn't fart or eat hay then she isn't interested".

Anne now takes the mockery in good humour, and once joked: "When I appear in public people expect me to neigh, grind my teeth, paw the ground and swish my tail."

In 1982, when the war broke out between Britain and Argentina over ownership of the Falkland Islands,

Prince Andrew served there as a helicopter pilot. He was given a job acting as a decoy for missiles, attracting some cruel jokes about his expendability. When he left for the South Atlantic, the Queen reacted exactly like any other mother. She contacted Rex Hunt, then Governor General of the Falklands, and asked him: "Do you think he'll be warm enough? Should we send him some extra clothing?"

Prince Andrew has had several high-profile love affairs, including one in 1982 with an American actress, Koo Stark, who had previously appeared in an erotic film. It was always said that royal disapproval prevented the young couple from marrying, but when the Queen saw a newspaper headline about "Andy and Koo", her only comment to them was: "Why don't they call you by your real names, Andrew and Katherine?"

Eventually, in 1986, Andrew married another commoner, Sarah Ferguson, a "PR executive" – a frequent job title for unmarried female London socialites. "Fergie" was pilloried by the press for her lack of royal sophistication. Prince Philip joined in the mockery. When Andrew and Sarah had a new house decorated to their tastes, Philip quipped: "It looks like a tart's bedroom." (Naturally, no one asked him how he would know.)

As heir to the throne, Charles was of course a very welcome baby. When the Queen's physician saw that her first-born child was a boy (in those days, there were no ultrasound scans to predict a baby's gender), he confessed that he had "never been so pleased to see a male organ in all [his] life." Since then, Charles has had a very long career as king-in-waiting, but joked about the lack of formal preparation for his eventual role as monarch, saying: "You pick it up as you go along. I learned the way a monkey learns, by watching its parents."

Very flattering for the Queen and Prince Philip.

Controlling the Grandchildren

The Queen seems to reserve some of her less humorous reactions for her grandsons William and Harry. Prince William, for example, has told the story of how he was once playing with his cousin Zara Philips (the daughter of Princess Anne) at Balmoral Castle, and made her crash into a lamppost while she was driving a go-kart. The Queen didn't laugh: William said that she came "running across the lawn in her kilt" and gave him "the most almighty bollocking."

In 2012, Prince Harry also did some hard playing, though in a more adult way. He was photographed naked while playing "strip pool" with women in Las Vegas. The Queen was reportedly furious and gave him a similar bollocking – behind closed doors. And when one of Harry's friends was implicated in a drug-smuggling plot, the Queen "ordered a full review of her grandson's inner circle".

When it comes to safety and the royal reputation, Elizabeth is as un-amused as Victoria ever was.

Where does she get it from? Well, as we have seen, the Queen grew up in a warm, loving household, and let's face it, they didn't have to face much hardship compared to the rest of the country, even during the depression of the late 1920s and the post-war years of rationing. So it's not surprising if they were generally good-humoured. But her family seems to have been genuinely fun-loving, especially compared to the photos we have all seen of her glum-looking great-great-grandmother Victoria.

However, we shouldn't set too much store by those old portraits of the glowering Victoria. Primitive early cameras produced blurred photos if the subject moved an eyelash. Sitters had to remain totally immobile for almost a minute. It's hardly surprising that Victoria, like almost everyone in 19th-century photos (sharp ones at least), looks stony-faced.

There have in fact been jokes bandied about the corridors of the family's palaces for generations, so that humour is something of a royal tradition.

Let's go back in time and look at a few predecessors who might have influenced the Queen ...

Queen Motherly Quips

The most immediate influence was naturally the Queen's own mother. She lived to the age of 101, but always seemed to preserve a youthful sense of fun. Once, in 1962, when she was into her own sixties, the Queen Mother danced the twist with politicians and aristocrats at a dinner party given by a minister who was later fired in a sex scandal.

She was also known for her risqué sense of humour. The harmonica player Larry Adler once gave a concert at the Queen Mother's home, Clarence House, and after the show, she asked to have a look at his mouth organ. He gave it to her and, in Adler's words, she winked at him and said: "No one will ever believe me when I tell them that I held Larry Adler's organ."

The Queen Mum had several gay men on her staff, and enjoyed both their company and their gossip about love affairs in the servants' quarters. Once, at a ball, she danced several times with one of her favourite gay male servants, who then excused himself and left the ballroom for a while.

When he came back, the Queen Mother teased him: "I hope you haven't been neglecting me in favour of the young men in the kitchen."

The Queen Mother was famous for enjoying the occasional glass of alcohol (followed by one or two more). One of her unofficial biographers wrote that she "floated on a sea of booze, never entirely sober, but never actually drunk."

She reputedly drank red wine with lunch, and if anyone asked for water, she would gasp: "How can you not have wine with your meal?"

With dinner, the Queen Mother would often drink Champagne, ideally Veuve Cliquot. Her favourite tipple, though, was an early-evening cocktail consisting of 30% gin and 70% Dubonnet, with a slice of lemon – a drink that has come to be known as a "Queen Mother".

All this alcohol doesn't seem to have damaged her health, and must have contributed to her famous geniality. The Queen Mother was well aware that people made fun of her drinking, and on one occasion, when she was served with a rather undersized glass of gin, she asked for more, saying "I've got my reputation to think of."

Even so, the Queen Mother knew how to control her drinking, and was conscious of the need to perform on public occasions. One lunchtime, seeing her daughter the Queen taking a large drink, the Queen Mother warned her: "Don't forget you've got to reign all afternoon."

The Queen Mother directly encouraged the Queen's own sense of levity. After the QM retired to a house on the north coast of Scotland, the Castle of Mey, the Queen often used to take a boat trip there on the royal yacht. As the Queen sailed away again, mother and daughter would exchange humorous poems. One of the Queen's verses thanked her mother for dinner:

"A meal of such splendour, repast of such zest,
It will take us to Sunday just to digest."

Older Generations of Royal Jokers

Going back a generation, the Queen's grandfather, George V, made a few quips that have been recorded for posterity. In particular, he is credited with some pithy sayings that must have been useful to his granddaughter. One of the most practical was "Always go to the bathroom when you have a chance." Today, the Queen's staff are always careful to programme what they call "health breaks" into her events.

On a similar theme, it is said that George V asked the aviator Charles Lindberg, the first man to fly the Atlantic flight, "What did you do about peeing?"

George V also expressed a sentiment that the modern royals have since echoed. He said that: "Once you've met one hundred and fifty lord mayors, they all begin to look the same."

George V was very particular about the British stamps that sported a picture of his head. When shown some of the first to be printed after he became king in 1910, he said, "they make me look like a stuffed monkey."

He was also a keen stamp collector, and one day his private secretary came to share a piece of philately news: "I see in *The Times* today that some damn fool has given fourteen hundred pounds for a single stamp at a private sale," the secretary said.

George V retorted, "I am that damn fool."

George V seems to have played a monumental practical joke on a shipbuilder. When in the early 1930s, the Cunard shipping line was planning to launch a giant new cruise liner, the plan was to call it *Victoria*. Until then, all Cunard's liners had names ending in "-ia" (*Mauritania, Aquitania*, etc). The head of Cunard told George V that he wished to name the new ship after "the greatest of all English queens."

George V replied: "Oh, my wife will be pleased," so Cunard had no choice but to christen the liner the *Queen Mary*.

Whether George V deliberately misunderstood or not, it was a highly effective reply, because the *Queen Mary* remained one of the world's most famous and prestigious cruise ships from its launch in 1936 until it was decommissioned in 1967. A great way to keep your wife happy.

Occasionally, George V also took a typically royal attitude towards the arts. When asked his favourite opera by the conductor Sir Thomas Beecham, George V replied, *La Bohème*, "the shortest one I know."

Even George V's last words were humorous – or so it is said. The most widely-told story is that when he was on his death bed, a doctor told him that he was getting better and would soon be well enough to visit the English seaside town of Bognor Regis. George V is said to have replied, "bugger Bognor". A neat bit of alliteration – a shame that it's almost certainly not true.

Going back another generation, Edward VII (Queen Elizabeth II's great-grandfather) made a famous remark that might have taught the Queen something about the dynastic nature of her job, where the death of a parent has to be shrugged of so that the monarchy can continue. As his mother Queen Victoria was on her deathbed, a member of the royal staff asked whether Edward thought she would be happy in heaven. He replied, "I don't know. She will have to walk behind the angels, and she won't like that!"

Edward VII was a fun-loving king, who enjoyed a little *too much* fun in Paris with actresses and prostitutes, according to his mother (for more details, see my book *Dirty Bertie, an English King Made in France*). Jokes in his household tended to be boisterous. He would pour brandy over the head of a courtier (who couldn't retaliate, of course); one Christmas, the mince pies served to his guests were full of mustard; Edward's mother Victoria was vehemently opposed to smoking, so he hung an "out of order" notice on a bathroom door so that he and his friends could hide in there and smoke.

When Edward VII was lying on his own deathbed in 1910, his wife Alexandra managed to make a jokey remark. Edward had been a life-long philanderer, and had even had "official" mistresses. So as he lay dying of lung disease brought on by his smoking, Alexandra told a friend, "now at least I know where he is."

Jumping back still further in the royal line, we come to Victoria, the queen who was so famously "not amused". It must be the best-known, and least humorous, royal quote ever (alongside Marie-Antoinette's "let them eat cake"), and in the popular imagination it sums up this dour, black-robed, haughty monarch. The legend is that Victoria would say "we are not amused" whenever someone tried to be funny in her presence, the plural "we" referring to herself and her dead husband Albert, and the "not amused" underlining the need to be serious while she was eternally mourning her departed prince.

In fact, though, it's likely that she never made the remark, or if she did, it was in a very specific context. The most convincing story is that her daughter Louise had become over-friendly with an aristocrat called Sir Arthur Bigge, who was known for his vulgar sense of humour. One evening at dinner, Bigge was telling smutty stories that were embarrassing everyone at table, so Victoria shut him up with the famous putdown: "We are not amused" – the "we" referring to everyone in the room except him.

Whether this is true or not, the saying became as well-known as Marie-Antoinette's (which she probably didn't say, either), and there is even a story (which, yet again, is probably apocryphal) about Victoria making fun of it herself. Supposedly, she was visiting a town in the north of England when the mayor said that he wanted to name a street after her. It was a small residential road, and the idea was to call it "Victoria Mews". Victoria is said to have replied, "We are happy to be a street, but we are not a mews."

(Yes, it sounds much too neat to be true.)

On the other hand, people who knew Victoria say that she really loved a good laugh. An English politician called Thomas Creevey described Victoria when she was young, writing in his memoirs that: "A more homely little being you never beheld when she is at her ease, and she is evidently dying to be always more so. She laughs in real earnest, opening her mouth as wide as it can go, showing not very pretty gums." (Well, half of the compliment was flattering.)

Victoria became more serious when she married her German husband, Albert, in 1840. He weaned her off frivolity and turned her into a moralizing Teutonic parent. Even so, the couple did retain a sense of fun –

in the bedroom at least. They fitted a mechanism by their bed so that they could press a button and bolt the door, allowing them to frolic uninterrupted. And when Victoria was told, after nine pregnancies, by her doctor that it would be better for her health to avoid a tenth, she replied: "Am I not to have any more fun in bed?"

In later life, contrary to her dour "un-amused" image, Victoria apparently regained her sense of humour. A typical product of the imperial age, she loved to listen to foreign dignitaries mangling the English language, and would sometimes have to stifle her laughter by hiding behind a handkerchief.

Like Elizabeth II and the modern royals, Victoria's taste in art and music was very conventional. Once, when she heard a piece of "modern" piano music, she asked what on earth it was. The pianist replied that it was a "drinking song", to which Victoria retorted, "Nonsense, you'd not drink a cup of tea to that!"

Victoria's uncle, George IV, was considered something of a joke as a king. Arrogant and overly fond of gambling, womanizing, building palaces, drinking and eating, he became a bloated sloth whom almost no one mourned when he died. The only quip he is credited with is, predictably, an insult. When he first caught sight of Caroline of Brunswick, the dowdy cousin he was to marry, he turned to a friend and said, "Harris, a glass of brandy ..."

Going even further back in the royal line, Charles II (who reigned from 1660-1685) was renowned as a wit.

He was once walking in London's Hyde Park with no protection other than two lords. His younger brother, James, drove by in a carriage, under heavy armed guard, and asked the King whether it was wise to walk about unprotected. Charles II replied: "No danger, for no man in England would take away my life to make you king."

In the 17th century, men still played women's roles in the British theatre. On one occasion, Charles II arrived to see *Hamlet*, only to be told that the performance would be delayed because the queen was being shaved. Charles exclaimed, "I beg her majesty's pardon! We will wait till her barber is done with her."

Charles II was also able to respond to criticism with a joke. His friend the Earl of Rochester once pinned a poem to his bedroom door:

"Here is our sovereign lord the king,
Whose promise no one relies on;
He never said a foolish thing,
Nor ever did a wise one."

Charles wrote back: "This is very true, for my words are my own, and my actions are those of my ministers."

It might sound flippant, but it's a reply that sums up the role of British constitutional monarchs. Fortunately for Britain, they can't do a thing without the permission of their ministers. It's the main reason why there is still a monarch today.

2 ROYAL ANIMALS

The Queen has always been fond of animals. Very, *very* fond, especially of dogs and horses. And her fondness can go way beyond the gourmet menus dished out to her corgis, who are said to dine on prime cuts of meat.

For example, in 1977 Sir Richard Sharples, the Governor General of Bermuda (which is a member of the Commonwealth), was gunned down while out walking his dog. The killer was arrested and sentenced to death, and appealed to Bermuda's head of state, the Queen, for clemency. She rejected the appeal, and allegedly commented: "He's got a cheek asking me. He even shot the dog." The sense of royal priorities is clear – assassinate a Governor General and you've got a chance of being spared. Kill the dog and you're doomed.

The Queen first became enamoured with dogs when her father bought himself a corgi in 1933, calling it "Dookie", a name based on his title at the time, the Duke of York. Young Princess Elizabeth fell in love with the breed, and since then she has owned about 30 corgis, all of them descendants of Susan, a dog she received as a present on her 18th birthday.

The Queen also keeps dorgis, a hybrid she created accidentally after a corgi mated with Princess Anne's dachshund, Pipkin. (It's surprising that the poor creatures have any legs at all.)

At home, the Queen is often photographed surrounded by corgis, but she also takes animals wherever she goes, in the form of lucky charms. She is very superstitious, and is said to carry miniature dogs and horses in her handbag as talismans. A case of "Dog Save the Queen"?

At home with the corgis (and dorgis)

As a young woman, Princess Elizabeth used to walk the corgis in St James's Park, near Buckingham Palace, disguised in a plain raincoat and headscarf (the Princess, that is, not the corgis). Given that the Palace has large grounds, one can only conclude that her parents sent her out to the park because they didn't want the dogs messing on the royal lawns.

Today, when the Queen is at one of her homes, she usually has a "morning tray" brought into her bedroom at 7:30am, with a pot of tea for her and a plate of biscuits for the dogs.

The dogs' dinner is served at 5:30pm, and just as human dinner guests are not allowed to start eating until the Queen herself begins her meal, so the dogs have to wait until she gives the order to tuck in.

On one occasion, the Queen was having tea with a group of clergymen. A footman brought in a tray of tea, with a plate of biscuits. A bishop didn't wait for the Queen's permission to start eating. He helped himself to a biscuit and took a bite. Only then did the Queen inform him that they were dog biscuits.

In 1999, the Queen demoted a footman when she found out that he had given whisky to one of the corgis as a joke.

Many of the rooms in the Queen's various homes have permanent stocks of soda water and absorbent paper in case the dogs disgrace themselves on the carpet. These soda siphons also come in handy if one of the corgis tries to bite a member of staff. Footmen are known to give irritable corgis a squirt of soda water to warn them off. They would never do it in front of the Queen, of course, but she is apparently perfectly accustomed to seeing one or more of her dogs dripping as if it's just taken a bath.

The Queen is unapologetic about the corgis' biting habits. She calls them "heelers", and says it's in their nature to "chase people". Once, a corgi bit a footman so hard on the leg that he dropped a tea tray. The Queen was apparently more worried about whether the dog had been scalded by falling tea than she was about the smashed cups or the holes in her footman.

In 2000, the Queen seems to have used the corgis to test a new recruit to her staff. She was interviewing Simon Walker as a potential press manager, when a corgi grabbed his trouser leg and started nibbling. The Queen carried on asking questions, and Walker, not knowing what to do, did nothing. He let the dog carry on chewing his trousers. And he got the job.

Prince Philip is also said to be less than enthusiastic about the corgis because of their high-pitched yapping. He got off to a bad start with the dogs because the Queen took her favourite corgi, Susan, on their honeymoon.

Princess Diana also used to hate the Queen's corgis, and said that the monarch was always surrounded by a "moving carpet" of dogs. Diana had a disastrous introduction to the Queen's canine army. On her first visit to the Queen's Scottish residence, Balmoral, with Charles, the new Princess burst into tears after seeing one of the dogs catch a mole. The Queen was highly amused by this, and on Diana's later visits, she would sometimes suggest they all go on a mole hunt.

Horse tales

The Queen has always been a keen rider, as well as an avid fan of horse racing. She owned her first horse when she was only four years old, a Shetland pony called Peggy that was given to her by her grandfather, King George V.

As a younger woman, she so enjoyed the experience of horse-riding that she didn't want to spoil it with a constrictive riding hat. When one of her horse trainers tackled her about her lack of head protection, she told him: "You don't have to have your hair done like I do." Consequently, she would often be seen galloping across a field wearing nothing more protective than a headscarf. Her staff used to joke that: "The only thing that comes between the Queen and her heir is a Hermès scarf."

Until 1986 the Queen used to attend the annual Trooping of the Colour parade (held in June to mark the sovereign's official birthday) on horseback, riding through the streets of London at age 60, taking the salute of her troops while perched on a precarious side-saddle. One hoot of a car horn or firework and she could have been galloping out of control across Trafalgar Square, or flat on her back outside Buckingham Palace. It goes to show how much she used to enjoy a ride with her soldiers.

As for horse racing, it seems to be a real royal passion. The most joyous photos of the Queen are taken when she is watching horse races – especially if one of her own mounts has just won. She has owned and bred racing thoroughbreds for most of her life, and even agreed to narrate a TV documentary about her equine activities in the 1970s. Her horses have won thousands of races (bringing in even more thousands of pounds in prize money), and she was champion flat-racing breeder in both 1954 and 1957. The Queen is, in short, a real figurehead and patron of the sport – a sort of David Beckham of horses.

She even made a horse-related joke during her coronation ceremony in 1953. When the Queen arrived at Westminster Abbey, one of her attendants asked whether she was feeling nervous. She replied,

"Of course I am, but I really do think Aureole will win." She was talking about one of her horses that was due to run in the Derby a few days later.

The Queen once joked about having to go to church regularly, as head of the Church of England: "If it weren't for my Archbishop of Canterbury, I should be off in my plane to Longchamp every Sunday". In fact, it might not have been a joke (even if there aren't races at Longchamp *every* Sunday).

The Queen's diary is sketched out 18 months in advance, and her staff know that the first thing they have to do in each year is put a line through six days in early summer – five to attend the Royal Ascot meeting in June, which opens every day with a royal procession, plus Epsom Derby Day, also in June. This is on top of at least a day at the annual Royal Windsor Horse Show in May or June. In the Queen's diary, even heads of state and archbishops take second place to horses.

Prince Philip is known to be less interested in horse racing than his wife. He preferred polo as a young man, and then moved on to carriage racing. When attending royal horse races, has been known to hide a miniature radio in his hat so that he can listen to the BBC's cricket commentary.

In the 1980s, one of Britain's most famous racing jockeys, Lester Piggott, was convicted of tax evasion, after (according to reports in the press at the time) paying his taxes with a cheque from a bank account that he had been concealing. Piggott was sent to prison for a year, and was stripped of his OBE. A journalist wrote to the Queen asking for this extra punishment to be overturned. The Queen refused the request, replying that: "He's not only been naughty, he's been stupid."

In 1991, the Queen arrived at the Royal Windsor Horse Show driving an ordinary Vauxhall car. She had just nipped across from the castle, which is next door to the park where the show is held. The security guard at the entrance to the VIP car park didn't recognize the woman at the wheel, and told her, "Sorry, love, you can't come in without a sticker." The Queen replied, "I think if you check, I'll be allowed to come in." The guard later told a reporter: "I thought she was some old dear who had got lost."

Speaking at the celebrations for her son Prince Charles's wedding to his long-time lover Camilla Parker-Bowles, the Queen expressed her happiness in pure racing terms. She said that the couple had overcome hurdles, like the horses in the Grand National, and now "my son is home and dry with the woman he loves. Welcome to the winner's enclosure."

The Queen has a lot of fun thinking up witty names for the horses she breeds. When one of her stallions called Lord Elgin mated with a mare called Amnesia, the Queen called the resulting foal Lost Marbles. A convoluted joke, but a clever one – Lord Elgin was the British aristocrat who, in the early 1800s, stole large segments of marble sculpture from the Parthenon in

Athens. Thanks to Britain's amnesia, the so-called Elgin Marbles have never been returned, and now reside in the British Museum, a situation that has predictably caused generations of Greek archaeologists to lose their marbles. All in all, a mischievous but effective bit of royal humour.

The Queen is highly protective of her horses. She once visited some stables where her racehorses were being kept, and decided that the stalls weren't getting enough ventilation. After the visit, she told the trainer, "it was incredibly dusty in there, and there was no air." To prove it, she blew her nose on a handkerchief and showed him the resulting dark patch. The ventilation was immediately upgraded.

The Queen is in horse racing to win. When her horse Free Agent won at Ascot in 2008, she shouted, "I've done it!" and punched the air like a footballer who's just scored a goal. When one of her mares, Estimate, won the Gold Cup in 2013, the Queen was pictured in newspapers patting the horse's nose with unbridled pride. The following year, Estimate came second in the same race. However, this time the joy was short-lived, because Estimate tested positive for morphine. Shock, horror! Had the Queen's racing team resorted to drugs in an attempt to snatch two wins in a row? No, the drug was traced to poppy seeds that had inadvertently got into the horse's feed. In the same period seven other horses were disqualified for the same reason. This was little consolation for the Queen, however, who had to return her £81,000 in prize money.

According to insiders, the Queen never bets on her own horses. Her racing advisor, John Warren, told a newspaper: "Her Majesty's gamble is on the breeding, using this stallion with that mare, hoping to produce something special." However, he did admit that she indulges in one gambling event. In the royal box on Derby Day, there's a sweepstake. Everyone selects a horse and puts a pound in the kitty. Potential winnings: about £16.

While the Queen Mother was alive, there were plenty of stories in the press about her gambling habits. In the most famous of these rumours, in 1985 she took a supersonic flight in Concorde to celebrate her 85th birthday, and spent part of the journey sitting in the cockpit, using the plane's radio to place bets on horses. Only after the Queen Mother's death in 2002 did her racing manager contradict the story, saying he was certain that "she never had a bet". She loved horse racing, he said, but what she loved almost as much were the untrue stories about her gambling.

If the Queen herself wanted to make money gambling on horse races, it would be all too easy. Every year, the bookmakers offer odds on what colour hat she will wear to Ascot. In the past, the odds have included 50-1 on her wearing the same hat as at her Jubilee celebrations, and 1000-1 on her sporting a Union Jack baseball cap, worn backwards.

So if the Queen ever has money troubles (which is highly doubtful), she just has to get a member of staff to go online and place a bet on the most unlikely headwear.

Other Animals

The Queen may be fascinated by dogs and horses, but she also has to take an interest in several surprising members of the animal kingdom, thanks to some of Britain's oldest and crankiest laws.

The Queen is, for example, legally the owner of any unmarked swans in British waters – and the only swans that get marked (with a nick in their beak) are those living on the Thames near Windsor Castle, so almost all newborn swans in Britain become *de facto* royal property. The law dates back to medieval times, when swan meat was a delicacy and was thought too refined to be gifted to the common people. This is probably why no one in modern Britain eats swan. The Brits have never got a taste for it, and they know they would be committing treason if they did.

The Queen has an official Swan Keeper, whose main job is to mark swans and send them out to foreign heads of state as gifts. Though once they reach their destination, there is no guarantee that they won't get eaten.

Most Brits know about the Queen's ownership of swans, but few are aware that she is also the legal proprietor of all "fishes royal". These are sturgeon, whales and dolphins. According to a 13th-century law, any of these "fishes" (back then, no one seems to have been aware of whales' and dolphins' mammalian status) that get washed up on British beaches belong to the monarch – although the Scots added a clause whereby any whales too heavy to be pulled ashore by six horses were not royal property.

Today, of course, most people try to help stranded whales or dolphins back out to sea, but in the past, they were valuable sources of meat, oil, and bones for corsets and umbrellas.

This ancient law about fish might seem quaint, but as recently as 2004, a fisherman called Robert Davies was threatened by police with six months in prison for selling a sturgeon he had caught in Swansea Bay.

Davies's defence was that he had faxed Buckingham Palace, offering the fish to the Queen, as the law required, and received royal permission to dispose of it as he wanted. Sadly for him, though, the wild sturgeon is an endangered species and also protected by modern British wildlife laws.

The royal status of sturgeon was confirmed yet again in 2013 when the Queen granted permission to a sturgeon farm in Cornwall to start producing caviar and smoked fish. Exmoor Caviar, which farms its fish at a secret location, is the only sturgeon farm in Britain – because it's the only one ever to get the royal seal of approval.

The Queen regularly receives gifts of animals when she goes on state visits. But she never keeps them – unless they are thoroughbred horses. In the past, these exotic gifts have included hippopotami, jaguars, beavers, an elephant and a crocodile. She passed all of them on, mainly to London Zoo. The crocodile was kept in her secretary's bathtub until the Zoo was ready to fetch it. Even a pure Siamese kitten was given away to a member of kitchen staff. As a pet, of course.

3 MEETING POLITICIANS

If there is one person on the planet who is conscious of politicians' temporary importance, and who is capable of reminding them of it, it is the Queen. During her reign, she has met 12 US Presidents, 13 British Prime Ministers, and hundreds of other heads of state.

In fact, when she heard the statistic about how many British Prime Ministers had served since she came to the throne, the Queen apparently corrected it, saying that the Commonwealth Prime Ministers should be included, pushing the number well over 100. She apparently views the Commonwealth leaders as the equals of her British PMs.

However this doesn't mean that the Queen takes all politicians seriously. She is known to be a good impressionist, and insiders say that she has done hilarious impersonations of, amongst others, Margaret Thatcher, Boris Yeltsin and Tony Blair.

British Prime Ministers

While still a young princess, Elizabeth used to meet British prime ministers, and always seems to have felt protective towards them. Once, in the spring of 1939, with the world on the brink of war, she was at a lunch with Neville Chamberlain (the naive PM who claimed to have negotiated "peace in our time" with Hitler in 1938) when a ladybird settled on the table. The 12-year-old princess declared that it brought good luck and said that it should be given to the Prime Minister. The insect was duly passed along the table and placed on Chamberlain's shoulder. Not that it brought him much luck – he was, of course, soon to be replaced by the more belligerent Winston Churchill.

Today, while the British parliament is in session, the Queen meets the Prime Minister every Tuesday evening at Buckingham Palace to discuss the political issues of the moment. No one else is present, and no records of the discussions are kept. The only witnesses are the corgis, of whom former PM John Major once said, "If they were bugged, all our State secrets would be apparent."

When Tony Blair revealed details of his discussions with the Queen in his memoirs, she is said to have been "deeply disappointed". And even though he was PM for ten years between 1997 and 2007, he has not been knighted.

Similarly, when David Cameron published his memoirs in 2019, he went into great detail about his meetings with the Queen to discuss the Scottish independence referendum of 2014. Panicking that the

Scots might vote to leave the United Kingdom, Cameron went to the Queen's residence in Balmoral, Scotland, and asked her to intervene (which was strictly against the rules governing the monarchy). Cameron claimed in his autobiography that he did not ask the Queen to do "anything that would be in any way improper ... but just a raising of the eyebrow even... a quarter of an inch." In the end, she agreed to give a televised speech, saying, "I hope people will think very carefully about the future", which was taken as a royal plea not to break up the Union. The Scots duly voted by about 53% to 47% to remain.

But by revealing these discussions, Cameron broke all the rules of protocol about a Prime Minister's dealings with the monarch. So it came as no surprise when a royal spokesperson was quoted in the press, saying that "it serves no-one's interests" for conversations between the PM and the Queen to be made public. "It makes it very hard for the relationship to thrive," they added. This is the Queen's equivalent of a slap in the face, so it is probably not advisable to bet on David Cameron receiving the royal summons to come to Buckingham Palace and get a knighthood.

As she has got older, the Queen has taken an increasingly maternal view of her Prime Ministers. She says that when they come to meet her, "they unburden themselves ... It's rather nice to feel that one's a sort of sponge." But this doesn't mean to say that she takes everything they say seriously. She has admitted that when she listens to a PM, "some things stay there and some things go out the other ear." Which is exactly how most British people feel about their politicians.

When Prince Charles and Princess Anne were small, the Queen moved the times of the Tuesday evening meetings with the Prime Minister to later, so that she could read her children a bedtime story first.

Margaret Thatcher admitted that the Queen had been an inspiration to her. After the Queen succeeded to the throne in 1952, Mrs T wrote that: "If, as many earnestly pray, the accession of Elizabeth II can help to remove the last shreds of prejudice against women aspiring to the highest places, then a new era for women will indeed be at hand." A blow for gender equality was obviously a great thing, but inspiring Maggie to forge her political career? Not all Brits would be grateful to the monarch for that ...

It is often said that the Queen and Margaret Thatcher didn't get on. Insiders noted that their relations seemed to be strained when Mrs T first came to power in 1979, because the Queen was put out by the new PM's mixture of bossy efficiency and excessive deference – apparently Mrs Thatcher used to curtsey much too low. Also, after one meeting, the Queen was heard to complain: "Mrs Thatcher never listens to a word I say."

The Queen was also irritated by Margaret Thatcher's voice. Mrs T was very conscious of her middle-class background, and used to put on an over-posh accent – which her own media advisors told her to tone down so that she would sound more human to the voters. The Queen apparently used to call Mrs Thatcher's accent: "Royal Shakespeare [Company] received pronunciation from circa 1950." (Which was, of course, what the Queen herself used to speak in the 1950s, though snobs would say that her pronunciation wasn't "received", it was inbred.)

The Queen used to tell a joke about Margaret Thatcher's irritating personality. It was a story about Mrs T visiting a retirement home. She goes to speak to an old man, who clearly has no idea why she is addressing him. Mrs T asks the old man (and here the Queen did a brutally accurate imitation of Thatcher's voice): "Do you know who I am?" And the old man answers: "No, but if you ask the nurse, she'll tell you."

Prime Ministers are sometimes invited on private visits to the Queen's Scottish home in Balmoral, and Mrs Thatcher was amazed to see the monarch getting up after dinner and clearing the table. Mrs T insisted on trying to help, but just got in the way, and the Queen muttered: "Will somebody please tell that woman to sit down?"

Mrs T was a very urban (or at least suburban) woman, and didn't feel at all at home visiting the Queen in rural Scotland. She used to arrive at Balmoral in heels, whereas the Queen's favourite footwear there was usually wellingtons. Someone once asked the Queen whether Mrs Thatcher enjoyed walking in the hills. "The hills?" the Queen exclaimed. "She walks on the road."

Mrs Thatcher's politics were more macho than many male Prime Minister's, but physically she did not have the Queen's resilience when it came to hours of standing during long ceremonies. At a reception in London for visiting diplomats, the Queen was amused to see that Mrs T had to go and sit down. The following year, at the same ceremony, Mrs Thatcher again felt light-headed, and had to be given a chair. The Queen turned to the Archbishop of Canterbury and said: "Look, she's keeled over again!"

In the 1980s, the Queen and Mrs Thatcher wore similar dresses to a function. Mrs T was horrified, and apologized to the Queen: "I'm so sorry. Next time we attend a function together, we must speak to each other to see what we are going to wear." The Queen dismissed this presumptuous suggestion, replying: "I never notice what anyone else is wearing."

Mrs Thatcher was PM from 1979 to 1990, so the two ladies had many Tuesday evening meetings, and eventually settled into an easier, friendlier relationship. Towards the end of Mrs T's tenure, they would prolong their meetings with a glass of whisky.

During the 1990s, then-Prime Minister John Major gave a private dinner for the Queen at 10 Downing St, inviting several former PMs. Ted Heath, who was in power from 1970-74, attended, but was old and frail, and nodded off during dinner, even though he was sitting next to the Queen. John Major told her: "Ted's fallen asleep." She replied, "I know he has," she replied, "but don't worry, he'll wake up a little later and we'll say nothing about it."

When Tony Blair came to Buckingham Palace after his election in 1997, he was only 43, the youngest Prime Minister since the Earl of Liverpool in 1812. As he walked forward to meet the Queen, Blair tripped over the carpet and almost grabbed at her hand. The Queen ignored the mishap, but seems to have been touched by this show of youthful clumsiness. She told Blair that he was her tenth Prime Minister: "The first was Winston. That was before you were born." It proves that she'd done her homework – Blair was born in 1953, just a year after she came to the throne and had her first prime-ministerial audience.

In the late 1990s and early 2000s, under the leadership of Tony Blair, Britain enjoyed a wave of optimism reminiscent of the 1960s. Blair seemed keen to claim the credit for this, prompting the royal family to nickname the self-important leader "President Blair". Hoping to appeal to young voters, Blair invited pop stars to Downing Street, and the press dubbed the nation "Cool Britannia."

However, the Queen had a longer-term, more historical view of Britain's symbolic figurehead, and complained to her cousin Margaret Rhodes, "Poor Britannia. She would have hated being cool."

The Queen's sense of mischief was accidentally revealed in all its glory during a banquet in 2008. Microphones picked up a conversation between the Queen and her daughter Princess Anne, with the monarch laughing about then-Prime Minister Gordon Brown, who had arrived late: "The Prime Minister got lost. He disappeared." The royal grin showed exactly how much respect she has for politicians.

And talk of disrespect brings us naturally to 2019's great fiasco – the clash between the Queen and probably the least respectful of all her Prime Ministers, Boris Johnson (which comes as something of a shock, given that he is a pure product of the Establishment, an Old Etonian, graduate of Oxford University and former pupil of the European School in Brussels).

Johnson has taken the traditional relationship between the reigning monarch and a British Prime Minister to a low that has surely not been seen since 1936, when Stanley Baldwin failed to convince King Edward VIII that the stability of his country in a time of desperate political threat was more important than marrying an American divorcée.

It has now become public knowledge, backed up by a Supreme Court ruling, that Boris Johnson "misled" the Queen in August 2019, when he asked her (or rather instructed her, because she cannot refuse) to prorogue (that is, suspend) parliament. Johnson allegedly claimed that the suspension was to prepare a Queen's Speech, though the usual period of parliamentary closedown in such cases is only a few days, not the five weeks that Johnson requested. The Supreme Court later ruled that prorogation was clearly an attempt to prevent parliamentary scrutiny of his plans to leave the EU, and MPs returned to

Westminster (and voted down Johnson's plan).

Even though the long prorogation was overturned, the Queen's Speech was retained, and this added royal insult to monarchic injury. The Queen's Speech (which is written for her by the government, and which she is constitutionally forced to read out) is usually given when parliament reconvenes after an election. It is therefore an announcement of what a new parliamentary majority is planning to do.

Johnson's speech, however, was to be given at a time when he had been chosen as leader by his party, rather than being elected, and when his majority in parliament was *minus* 45. He therefore had almost zero chance of getting any of his policies voted through. He was in fact, in the process of being the least successful Prime Minister ever, having lost *every single one* of the votes in parliament during his term of office.

So the speech that the Queen gave on 14 October 2019 was not a realistic government agenda. Instead, coming just before an expected general election, it was viewed as a party political broadcast in favour of Boris Johnson. The Queen had been used as part of his election campaign. It came as no surprise that she read out the speech in a croaky voice, as though her vocal cords were rebelling against this abuse of parliamentary power. Nor that she read it with both eyebrows raised, as if punctuating every sentence with a silent "what!?".

The speech was a serious breach of constitutional rules, and a mark of astonishing disrespect towards

British institutions from the Conservative Party (the irony is in the name), and specifically from Boris Johnson. So for once the Queen probably has no sense of humour about the matter. When Johnson promises that, unlike David Cameron, he will reveal nothing about his conversations with the Queen, it is probably because they are frosty affairs during which she shows all too clearly that she doesn't believe a word he is saying.

There is, though, the chance of a killing royal joke here. Constitutionally, the Queen has the power to ask any elected Member of Parliament (usually the head of a party) if he or she might be able to form a majority government. If this is done when there has not recently been an election – when, for example, a Prime Minister is in minority government, as is the case for Boris Johnson – it would mean that the Queen is implicitly sacking the PM. Yes, in theory at least, the Queen could ask an MP to boot Boris out of his job. It would be an historic punchline – the last time it was done was in 1834, when King William IV unseated Lord Melbourne as head of the government. But some would argue that these are extraordinary times, and the nation is in serious need of a joke.

Your Majesty, the choice is yours.

Politicians' gaffes

Traditionally, ordinary British stamps have nothing on them except the Queen's head and a price. In March 1965, the left-wing politician Tony Benn, who was serving as Postmaster General, came to see the Queen at Buckingham Palace, hoping to persuade her that these purely royal stamps were out-dated and elitist. He brought along a sheaf of designs for new stamps without the Queen's head. In his diary, he described how he gave her a long lecture, and then spread his designs all over the floor, getting down on his knees to comment on each one. He was sure, he said, that his "charm" had "done the trick".

However, when he reported back to the Prime Minister, Harold Wilson, the latter simply asked: "Did she get down on the floor with you?"

And in fact, it became evident that the Queen had let Mr Benn perform his pantomime, but had absolutely no intention of heeding him. Benn duly received a royal letter asking him not to commission any more "headless" designs.

Tony Benn was quickly re-assigned to a new post as Minister of Technology. When he came to the Queen to be sworn in, she joked, "I'm sure you'll miss your stamps."

In 1974, when Prime Minister Harold Wilson submitted a list of names for the honours list, the Queen saw that he wanted her to ennoble a close female friend of his. She disapproved, but protocol forbade her from intervening directly. Instead, she sent the PM a message saying: "Mr Wilson does know that if he wants to change anything, he can do so right up until the last minute?" (He didn't change his mind, and the Queen let the lady become a Lady.)

In 1981, Prince Charles proposed to visit Gibraltar, the disputed British territory on the coast of Spain, during his honeymoon cruise with Princess Diana. The Queen was advised that the visit might be controversial. In reply, she is said to have exclaimed: "He's my son, it's my yacht, and it's my colony!"

During a meeting of the Privy Council (a group of senior politicians who advise the Queen on political matters), Labour MP Clare Short's mobile phone rang. Embarrassed, Ms Short didn't dare answer. When the ringing stopped, the Queen said: "Oh, dear, I hope it wasn't anyone important."

Dealing with the Commonwealth

Australia still has the Queen as its head of state, and has a British Governor General. This causes some tensions, and there have often been calls for Australia to leave the Commonwealth and become a republic. During the 1970s, the Australian Prime Minister, Gough Whitlam, was known to be a staunch republican. When he came to Britain on a state visit in 1972, he brought the Queen a present – a sheepskin rug. The Queen was delighted. She put it on the floor and lay down on it, stroking the fleece and saying how beautifully soft it was. The Queen's press secretary Martin Charteris described the occasion bluntly: "That evening she was quite determined to catch her man. A lot of her sexuality has been suppressed, but that night she used it like a weapon ... It was an arrant use of sexuality. I was absolutely flabbergasted."

Instantly falling under the Queen's spell, thereafter Whitlam became a much less vocal republican.

On one occasion, a delegation of Australian politicians were having tea with the Queen and Prince Philip at Buckingham Palace, discussing the thorny issue of republican sentiments amongst certain Australians. Ever the *gaffeur*, Prince Philip made a remark that annoyed the Australians. The Queen instantly apologized and told Philip: "You don't know what you're talking about." The Australians calmed down and discussions continued amicably.

The Queen takes an active, and often passionate, interest in the welfare of the Commonwealth: in 1977, during her Silver Jubilee celebrations, she expressed her relief that Idi Amin, the infamous President of Uganda, would not be coming. If he had turned up, she told Earl Mountbatten, she would have used London's ceremonial Pearl Sword at St Paul's Cathedral "to hit him hard over the head".

In 1979, the Queen was due to go on an African tour when Rhodesia declared independence and renamed itself Zimbabwe. This only came about after a long and bitter colonial war that also involved Zambia (Zimbabwe accused Zambia of harbouring anti-independence guerrillas). The Queen was due to visit Zambia during her tour, and some of her advisors thought that she should stay well clear of the war zone. The Queen scoffed at this suggestion and told her security people: "Of course I'm going. You can see that I don't get shot." The tour went ahead as planned, and on 28 July 1979, the Queen, Prince Philip and their son Prince Andrew were warmly welcomed by crowds in Lusaka, Zambia.

Don't Touch the Queen!

As a younger woman, the Queen enjoyed Scottish dancing, and has been filmed skipping around the dance floor with various kilted males. But on formal occasions, physicality is taboo. Normally, protocol dictates that the only physical contact allowed with the Queen during a formal ceremony, even for heads of state, is a handshake. She may be a modern monarch in some ways, but the Queen does not do high fives or hugs – except perhaps with members of her family.

This explains why the British press gets very annoyed when some foreign leader gets uppity and attempts uncalled-for intimacy with the monarch. The Queen herself usually remains calms in such situations, but then she's not likely to punch some other country's president for having wandering hands.

In 1992, then Australian Prime Minister Paul Keating created a media furore when he began introducing the Queen to reception guests while holding an arm halfway up the monarch's back, as though they were dancing partners. Infuriated British tabloids dubbed him "the Lizard of Oz".

In 2000, when the Queen got up the courage to return Down Under, the new Prime Minister John Howard appeared to make exactly the same *faux pas*, but photos of his arm showed that it was actually hovering a few centimetres behind the Queen's back. To make this completely clear, his office issued a statement, insisting that: "We firmly deny that there was any contact whatsoever."

In April 2004, the Queen went to Paris to celebrate the centenary of the Entente Cordiale, the treaty allying France and Britain. However, French President Jacques Chirac got a little too cordial, and as he accompanied the Queen on a walkabout in the streets of Paris, he couldn't stop touching her, his hands frequently gripping her arm and even straying to her back. The Queen appeared indifferent to this unwanted attention, but back home, the *Daily Mail* was shocked, and reported that: "The French leader's hand frequently went to her shoulder and, at one stage, hovered in a guiding gesture almost level with her waist." The paper headlined its article "Hands Off!" and said (half-seriously) that: "It could have caused more damage to relations than Waterloo." Whether they meant the battle or the naming of the London railway station wasn't clear.

When the Obamas came to London for the 2009 G20 summit, the naturally ebullient First Lady, Michelle, ignored protocol at the evening reception and clasped the Queen with an affectionate arm, her hand resting almost on the monarch's shoulder. To many people's surprise, the Queen responded with an arm around Michelle's waist, albeit a rather limp, tentative embrace. But then the Queen is not used to public displays of affection. Especially not with Americans.

In July 2017, David Johnston, Governor of Canada, had to issue a public explanation after he was seen giving the Queen's left elbow the lightest of touches during Canada's 150th anniversary celebrations in London: "I'm certainly conscious of the protocol," Johnston told a TV journalist. "I was just anxious to be sure there was no stumbling on the steps. It's a little bit awkward, that descent to Trafalgar Square, and there was carpet that was a little slippy, so I thought perhaps it was appropriate to breach protocol just to be sure there was no stumble." Oh well, maybe, just maybe, in that case, it's acceptable for a Canadian to touch Her Majesty. But only once every 150 years.

The most successful attempt by a politician at making the Queen loosen up and get physical was probably made by Nelson Mandela in July 1996. They were in the royal box at the Albert Hall in London, attending a concert entitled "Two Nations Celebrate", featuring both British and African performers. When the South African choral group Ladysmith Black Mmbaza began to sing, Nelson Mandela stood up and started to dance. Prince Philip was the first to get out of his seat to accompany Mandela, followed by Charles. Then, to many people's surprise, the Queen joined in, though her dancing was restricted to a subdued regal swaying.

A warm royal welcome

The Queen is, of course, a veteran at receiving foreign leaders, all of whom crave the prestige of being photographed with the most famous lady on the planet when they come to Britain.

The Queen is acutely conscious that during these visits, hers is a symbolic role. She is not there to sign political alliances. She has said that when she and Prince Philip invite a world leader for bed and breakfast at Windsor Castle or Balmoral, "we are the hosts, basically. I mean, we give the entertainment. We have them to stay, hoping to give them a nice time to remember." She almost sounds as though she is hoping for good reviews on Tripadvisor.

Of their banquets, she takes an equally modest view: "We put on our best clothes and everybody dresses up. And the best glass and china and the gold plate comes out." But, she adds, "it's worth explaining that we do put it on specially and we don't live like this all the time." She clearly doesn't want to be compared to monarchs of the past like Louis XIV – or, for that matter, with modern French presidents who live in a palace and eat most meals off France's best porcelain.

Usually these visits by foreign leaders go well, and the Queen is careful to prevent any *faux pas* being made in her name. For example, when the King and Queen of Thailand came to Britain in 1960s, she was afraid that the army band that was due to play at the welcoming ceremony might make a rather obvious, but indelicate, choice of music. She therefore sent a note to the organizers saying: "Tell the band leader under no circumstances to play excerpts from *The King and I*".

In 1976, the Queen was especially keen for the visit by French president Valéry Giscard d'Estaing to go well. Britain and France were co-operating on the supersonic plane, Concorde, but Giscard was apparently convinced that the Brits were losing enthusiasm for the costly project. The Queen took it upon herself to change his mind. Giving a speech during a banquet at Buckingham Palace, she told her press secretary Martin Charteris to applaud loudly as soon as she mentioned Concorde. He did so, and other British guests immediately started to follow suit.

Next day, Giscard told reporters that this "loud and spontaneous applause" had convinced him that Britain was fully behind Concorde. Royal mission accomplished.

However, the Queen occasionally shows a less hospitable sense of humour when greeting foreign heads of state ...

In September 1998, Crown Prince Abdullah of Saudi Arabia visited the Queen at Balmoral for lunch. After the meal, the Queen asked her guest whether he would like a tour of her Scottish estate. The Crown Prince accepted the invitation, and got into the Land Rover that was parked in front of the castle, while his interpreter sat behind him. To their surprise, the Queen herself got into the driving seat. At that time, women were forbidden from driving in Saudi Arabia, a fact that the Queen surely knew, so one can imagine the Saudi's unease. And his discomfort was only just beginning ...

The Queen learned to drive during the Second World War, and apparently practises a rather military style of driving around the Balmoral estate. As her cousin Margaret Rhodes put it: the Queen drives "like a bat out of hell", and she doesn't believe in seat belts.

And on this particular day, as well as speeding along the narrow lanes that she knows so well, the Queen appeared to be only half-concentrating on her driving, as she was giving a running commentary on everything they were seeing.

The rattled Crown Prince told his interpreter to suggest that it might be best to slow down, but the Queen cheerfully carried on accelerating through the countryside, taking her hands off the wheel to point out things of interest.

Later, a Saudi spokesman commented: "I am sure she steers the ship of state more steadily than she drives a Land Rover."

It's easy to imagine the Queen having a giggle about her practical joke afterwards, but the awkward question is: did her prank make the Saudis determined to deny women the right to drive for so many years afterwards?

Former US President George Bush Senior came to visit the Queen at Buckingham Palace after he had left office. As they talked, Mr Bush noticed a three-legged silver dish and asked the Queen what it was for. She replied: "I was hoping you could tell me. You gave it to me."

The visit to London in March 2008 by France's President Nicolas Sarkozy seems to have been planned according to the Queen's sense of humour. Either that, or she was completely unaware of the details of the arrangements – which seems very hard to believe.

When Monsieur Sarkozy arrived to meet the Queen at Windsor Castle, he was greeted by a pair of horse-drawn carriages. The first was for the French President and the Queen, the second for their spouses, Carla Bruni-Sarkozy and Prince Philip. As the two couples rode to the castle, they were escorted by the Household Cavalry, whose uniform includes breastplates that are copies of the ones stolen from dead French soldiers at Waterloo. Not exactly diplomatic. Admittedly, this detail may not have occurred to the Queen, but, given her love of horses, she would surely have known that two of the cavalry horses accompanying her on that day were called Agincourt (the battle at which English archers massacred French nobles in 1415) and Zut Alors.

The series of *faux pas* continued at the castle. To reach the royal banquet that evening, French and British guests had to pass through an antechamber called the Waterloo Room, which is decorated with portraits of the battle's two victors, the Duke of Wellington and Field Marshal Blücher. And this was only an *hors d'oeuvre* for what was about to happen.

The banqueting table was laid for 160 guests, and it is surely impossible to believe that the Queen had not been consulted when the dinner service was chosen. She must have known that Monsieur Sarkozy, the French ambassador and countless other French dignitaries would be sitting down to eat off a huge

Sèvres porcelain service that was bought by the British royal family just after the French Revolution, when the contents of the royal Chateau de Versailles were sold off on the cheap. In other words, the French delegation had been invited to the Queen's home and given dinner on what was essentially a plundered French national treasure.

It's hardly surprising that Monsieur Sarkozy cut his visit to Windsor short and left for France the next day – no doubt leaving the Queen to chuckle at her historical jokes.

In case French readers think that the Queen might be just another British exponent of the ancient sport of French-bashing, there are a couple of stories that might re-assure them.

In May 1972, while visiting France, a year before Britain joined the European Union, the Queen gave a highly diplomatic speech, summing up Anglo-French relations with an analogy: "We may drive on different sides of the road, but we're going the same way." (This is of course illegal and highly dangerous, but the Queen clearly thought it was a metaphor that the French, those famously reckless drivers, would understand.)

Decades later, at a state banquet with President François Hollande in June 2014, the Queen gave a speech in both French and English. In her *très anglais* accent, she said that the British and the French enjoy a unique relationship – "d'amitié, de rivalité dans la bonne humeur, ainsi que l'admiration" (friendship, good-humoured rivalry, and admiration). She even came up with rather a clever pun in French, calling the English Channel "non pas une ligne de partage, mais un trait d'union" – not a line of partition but a hyphen, in French, literally a "line of union".

Of course we can't be sure that she wrote the pun herself, but her dead-pan delivery was perfect, in the tradition of the best British stand-up comedians.

4 THE PUBLIC PERSONA

Thanks to her coronation, her jubilees, Christmas Day speeches, state visits and various royal weddings (including her own), the Queen's countless TV appearances have probably attracted the biggest combined audience figures in the history of the small screen.

In 1953, for example, over 20 million Britons watched her coronation on TV – this might not sound very impressive by today's standards, but it wasn't bad considering that there were only 2.7 million television sets in the whole country. By the time she (or a stuntman) parachuted out of a helicopter with James Bond during the opening ceremony of the 2012 London Olympics, the Queen was attracting an estimated 900 million viewers around the world. Again, not the biggest viewing figures ever, but the Queen's big-occasion appearances have regularly been notching up similar statistics for more than 60 years.

She must also be the most widely-travelled head of

state in world history. She began scaling back her heavy travel schedule at the end of the 20th century, but during her long reign she has been to more than 100 countries on over 250 state visits, and has probably shaken hundreds of thousands of hands.

Of course, travel arrangements are never particularly arduous for the monarch. When going abroad, she doesn't even have to remember to take her passport – because she doesn't have one. And it would be pretty pointless anyway, seeing that the message on the inside cover of a British passport "requires all those whom it may concern to allow the bearer to pass freely … in the name of Her Majesty". She might as well tell everyone in person.

Only once has this caused problems. In 1984, the Queen was briefly denied entry to the USA when a female customs and immigration official demanded to see a passport – she recognized the Queen but needed to see proof of ID. It took a phone call to Washington to convince the customs lady that the Queen wasn't an illegal immigrant.

The Queen's travels haven't been limited to glamorous world tours. Throughout her reign, she has visited every corner of the British Isles, and has got so used to these domestic trips that she describes them as her "away days", as if she were a pensioner getting a cheap ticket to Brighton.

The Queen knows that every instant of her long career of visiting buildings, accepting flowers and waving to crowds has been under scrutiny, with the press looking on and spectators seeking to etch the historic occasion on their memory. As she once confided to the Dean of Windsor: "My father told me that whatever I said or did, to anyone, they would remember it."

The problem with this constant scrutiny is the need to look both regal and simultaneously benevolent. In her early reign, the Queen confessed that she "assumed people wanted her to look solemn most of the time." Since then she has said that she feels she often looks too glum, a sort of live version of the unsmiling portraits on coins, banknotes and stamps. She has complained that: "I don't have a naturally smiley face". When seen in public she is either concentrating on the proceedings (and therefore looking very formal) or being genuinely, spontaneously amused by something, at which time she will crack a real smile or laugh. There is nothing in between, because she doesn't do the forced celebrity grin for the cameras.

If there are any hitches in protocol, the Queen is careful not to react with more than her famous stare, which usually lasts no more than a second, the time it takes for the stare to hit the recipient between the eyes. In this, she is unlike her sister Margaret, who was more openly snooty than the Queen herself. Once, when someone addressed Margaret as "Your Highness", instead of "Your Royal Highness", she apparently blurted out: "There are members of Arab states who are highnesses. I am a royal one." There is probably a reason why Princess Margaret didn't often go on state visits to the Middle East.

The Queen, on the other hand, is always careful to make a good impression, as a symbol of her nation should. To give tangible proof that she wishes everyone well, she therefore engages in small talk with members of the public, the danger being that this can lead to embarrassingly dull conversations being recorded for posterity. When visiting Niagara Falls, for example, the Queen, desperately grasping for something to say, was heard to utter: "It looks very damp".

Fortunately, her public appearances often produce much better repartee than that …

Meeting the people

The Queen was trained in the royal art of waving by her grandmother, Queen Mary, the wife of George V. The royal wave has been described as holding up your hand and moving it side to side, as if caressing an invisible buttock.

Even as a small girl, Elizabeth was seen waving very regally from the balcony of Buckingham Palace. The infant Princess also passed on some of the advice about public appearances to her younger sister. Elizabeth once told Margaret: "If you see someone with a funny hat, you must not point at it and laugh."

The Queen performed her first solo official engagement as a 17-year-old. She was so nervous that one of her mother's ladies in waiting gave her a barley sweet to calm her down.

As a young woman, the Queen wasn't always diplomatic about her trips to the British provinces. In 1957, she was reading the draft of a speech that she was due to give in the tough northern port of

Kingston-upon-Hull. It opened with the line: "I am very happy to be in Kingston today." The Queen said that she wanted it changed: "I will be pleased to be in Kingston, but I will not be *very* pleased." These days, she wouldn't dare be that honest.

When the Queen is due to greet a line of mayors and councillors wearing their chains of office, she says that she are going to meet the "chain gang".

Sometimes, when the Queen meets members of the public, the scope of the occasion goes far beyond than the chance to wave flags at an English lady in a hat. In 1956, during a visit to Nigeria, the Queen visited the Oji River leper settlement. She had been told that the local people did not believe leprosy could be cured, and were shunning or abusing former sufferers who were in fact clear of the disease. As a gesture of solidarity, the Queen shook hands with cured lepers to show that she had faith in medical progress. (This was, incidentally, some 30 years before Princess Diana achieved virtual sainthood status by shaking the hand of an AIDS patient.)

On a visit to Scotland, the Queen saw that her Lord-Lieutenant, Lord Clydesmuir, was stuck in the official limousine. He had got his sword jammed, and couldn't get out the door.

Initially the Queen sympathized with his predicament, while a row of people stood waiting for the Lord-Lieutenant to introduce them to her.

Finally, she lost patience. Marching towards the greeting line, she announced: "My Lord-Lieutenant appears to be having difficulty in getting out of the car, so I'd better introduce myself. I'm the Queen."

During the euphemistically-named "troubles" in Northern Ireland, the British royal family was not exactly popular amongst certain members of the province's population. In 1977, for example, there was a demonstration against her visit, at which republican protesters carried a banner marked "Queen of Death". Even so, the Queen went through with her tour of Northern Ireland, on one occasion visiting a university where a bomb had exploded a week earlier.

However, it was before the "troubles" really began that the Queen suffered her only attack. In 1966, a 17-year-old Irish republican threw a four-kilo breeze block from six floors up, aiming for the glass sunroof of the royal Rolls. He failed to drop the piece of masonry on the Queen's head, but hit the front of the car as it drove slowly past.

After recovering from the initial shock, the Queen commented: "It's a strong car."

During a trip to New Zealand in 1986, of which the Queen is still head of state, two women threw eggs at the royal car, one of which smashed on the Queen's pink coat. At first upset by the attack, the Queen later quipped: "I myself prefer my eggs for breakfast."

In 2007, the Queen gave a reception for 350 prominent Americans in London. As she was talking to some sportsmen, a pushy man interrupted their conversation. "Do you play football?" the Queen asked him. "No," he said, "I sell pancake and waffle mix." The Queen shook her head and said: "How interesting what people will eat." The lesson: don't interrupt the Queen's conversations.

When the Queen first visited New York in October 1957, she specifically asked to approach the city from the harbour, because it was a view she had always dreamt of seeing. When she first caught sight of the Manhattan skyline from a US Army boat, she exclaimed "weee!" (apparently the royal equivalent of "wow!"), and said that the gleaming glass buildings reminded her of "a row of great jewels". Not a comparison that might occur to all of us, but then she probably possesses jewels that size.

At the end of that visit to New York, the Queen and Prince Philip drove straight from a ball to the airport. The inside of their limousine was lit up so that spectators could see the Queen ride by in her tiara. However, it was the early hours of the morning, so some people were standing on their balconies in pyjamas and nightdresses. The Queen turned to Philip and said: "I certainly wouldn't come out in my nightclothes to see anyone drive by, no matter who it was!"

But then New York in early autumn is a lot warmer than London.

In May 2007, the Queen went to Jamestown, Virginia, the first British colony established in the future USA. In the museum she stopped by an iron implement that was labelled as a spatula "for severe constipation". She showed it to her travelling doctor

and told him: "You should have something like that."
(A comment, perhaps, about American food?)

In 1992, there was a terrible fire at Windsor Castle, causing massive damage to the Queen's apartments, the State Dining Hall and the chapel. The renovation work lasted five years, and on its completion (six months early), the Queen gave a party for 1,500 workers who had done the rebuilding. During the celebration, a Pakistani carpenter broke protocol and told the Queen: "Your Majesty, please come with me. I want you to meet someone." She followed him and was introduced to his brother. He then took her to meet yet another of his brothers, who had also carved some of the woodwork. The Queen happily said hello, though she later confided to an Indian diplomat: "I began to worry that he might have twelve brothers."

In June 2014, the Queen visited the set of *Game of Thrones* in Belfast. Shown the series' famous iron throne made out of more than 1,000 swords, she was invited to try it out, but refused, saying that it looked "uncomfortable". When asked whether the Queen had declined the offer because she watched the show, and therefore knew that one of the kings who sat on it was poisoned, Buckingham Palace refused to confirm that the series was ever watched in the royal household. Which probably means no – after all, the Queen has her own real-life games of thrones to deal with.

Wherever she goes, the Queen gets presented with bouquets of flowers. At the 2016 Chelsea Flower Show, British's prime annual gardening event, she was talking to a herbalist, who told her that lily of the valley used to be used as poison. The Queen replied, "I've been given two bunches this week. Perhaps they want me dead."

Occasionally, when the Queen is on a visit, not everyone knows that there's a royal in town. Once, in Scotland, she greeted a member of the public who told her she looked just like the Queen. The monarch replied: "How re-assuring."

When meeting the public, the Queen usually asked banal questions like "do you live here?" or "have you been waiting long?" But once, a member of the public got in first with a much more pertinent (or impertinent) question, and asked the Queen: "What do you do?" The Queen later admitted to a friend, "I had no idea what to say."

The Queen showed a similar modesty in 2011 when she went to a party given by her cousin Lady Elizabeth Anson, who runs a company called Party Planners (their first event was a disco for the teenaged Prince Charles). At the party, the Queen mixed with Lady Elizabeth's employees, including cooks and flower-arrangers. Afterwards, she said, "Everybody was so friendly to me."

Prince Charles and the Queen were driving to the race course at Ascot in an open carriage. Charles heard a shout from the crowd, and asked his mother what had been said. The Queen did a perfect impression of a Cockney accent: "Gizza wave, Liz," she said, waving.

In May 1991, the Queen went on a state visit to the USA, and was greeted at the White House by President George Bush Senior, who gave his speech of welcome. The Queen then stepped up to the same podium to reply, but it had been adjusted for Mr Bush's height, and he had forgotten to place a step for her to stand on. The result was that the Queen was almost invisible behind the lectern. Press photos showed just a pair of eyes and a hat. Next day, she gave a speech to Congress, and began it by saying: "I do hope you can see me today".

In March 1983 the Queen and Prince Philip visited California, and were invited to the ranch belonging to President Ronald Reagan. It was a very rainy day, and the road to the mountain ranch was barely passable, but the Queen insisted on going. When she and Philip got there, they were treated to a warm fire piled with logs that Reagan had cut himself. He also gave them a western-style meal of enchiladas and re-fried beans. The Queen tucked in heartily, and told the President: "That was so enjoyable. Especially the used beans."

At the end of her visit, after six days' of non-stop rain, the Queen gave a speech at which she said: "I knew before we came that we had exported many of our traditions to the United States, but I had not realized before that weather was one of them."

Having fun during ceremonies

Even the Queen's solemn coronation ceremony on 2 June 1953 was punctuated by jokey comments. As she was about to proceed along the aisle of through

Westminster Abbey, with her maids of honour holding the train of her dress, she turned to them and said, "Ready girls?"

The royal robes were so heavy that she even asked the Archbishop of Canterbury to give her a push, saying: "Get me started."

The Archbishop created something of a flutter himself during the ceremony. After anointing the Queen's hands and forehead with holy oil, he also painted the sign of the cross on the young monarch's bare *décolleté*. It was a gesture that the previous Queen, Victoria, had forbidden.

When the newly anointed Queen joined her husband Prince Philip after the ceremony, wearing her crown, Philip greeted her with: "Where did you get that hat?" (This was the title of a famous English musical hall song – appropriately, about a man who is forced to wear his grandfather's hat in order to inherit his money.)

When the Queen opens each session of Parliament, she wears the Imperial State Crown. However, it is usually on show at the Tower of London, so for rehearsals, she sometimes parades around carrying a bag of flour on her head.

The crown travels alone to the Houses of Parliament in its own carriage, and the Queen insists that as it travels, the great jewels that the crown contains should face forwards for symbolic reasons. She gave a newly-appointed crown jeweller a tip on how to remember this, telling him: "The horses are always in front of the carriage."

The Queen has to look very formal during ceremonies, but this doesn't stop her taking them lightly. In a recent documentary she was filmed waiting to enter the very official Diplomatic Reception at Buckingham Palace, at which she meets all the London ambassadors and chief members of their staff. Standing in the antechamber in all her finery, waiting for the doors to be opened so that she could meet the 800 assembled guests, she turned to the Lord Chamberlain and said: "Do you think there will be anyone there?"

During official functions, the Queen likes to keep things moving. As a young woman, she would sometimes prod her mother on the ankle with an umbrella if she slowed down during a visit.

And it was in a spirit of time-saving that the Queen once gave out the wrong medals to a whole group of award recipients. While waiting for an honours ceremony to start, a member of her staff dropped the medals that were about to be awarded. Unfortunately, they had all been laid out in the order that the recipients were to be presented to the Queen. Seeing the chaos, she shrugged and said that she would pin the medals on the wrong chests: "I'll give them anything and you can sort it out afterwards."

For the Queen's Silver Jubilee celebrations in 1977, an enormous firework display was planned in Windsor Great Park. Unfortunately, as the evening began, everything started to go awry. First the bonfire started too early, before the Queen had had a chance to light it officially. After this, a flare was meant to go up, marking the start of the main firework display. Instead, there was a huge explosion, as some of the fireworks went off prematurely. The man in charge of the pageant, Sir Michael Parker, apologized to the Queen: "Your Majesty, I'm afraid it's all going terribly wrong." She replied: "Oh good. What fun."

At official banquets, the Queen usually follows a strict pattern of conversation. For the first part of the meal, she talks to the person on her left. Everyone else is expected to do the same. For the second half, she swivels to the right. Guests are always briefed about this protocol so that no one is left talking to the back of a head. But the Queen is attentive to other aspects of official dining, too. She once pointed out to a dinner guest that some people had their napkin wrong side up in their laps. "They're doing it all wrong," she said. "They've got the starched side down. The napkin will slip off their knees. You do it like this – the unstarched side on your lap and then you tuck it under your bottom." (This is, incidentally, one of the few occasions when the Queen has publicly acknowledged the existence of a royal bottom.)

On official occasions, the Queen often travels through the streets of London in a horse carriage, with a cavalry escort. During one such procession, one of the soldiers on horseback was riding right alongside the carriage window, so the Queen leaned out and gently told him: "Captain, I think it's me they've come to see."

Meeting Celebrities

The Queen is, of course, one of the biggest celebrities on the planet. But she is fundamentally unlike other celebrities, and not only because she doesn't attend reality TV stars' birthday parties or get into Twitter slanging matches.

The Queen exists outside the celebrity world. She watches films and television, and goes to the theatre – she even gets to meet the stars after the show – but she doesn't follow trends, so there's always a chance that when she meets someone incredibly famous, she won't have a clue who they are. For example, in 2005 she asked the 1960s guitar hero Eric Clapton, "Have you been playing a long time?"

However, the Queen does have her favourite stars, and a meeting with them can often produce a touch of regal wit.

In 1991, the British actress Prunella Scales played the Queen in the television version of Alan Bennett's play *A Question of Attribution*. Shortly after the screening, the Queen was introduced to the actress, who bowed to her. The Queen quipped: "I expect you think I should be doing that to you."

When British stand-up comedian Tommy Cooper met the Queen, he broke protocol by asking her a question before she addressed him:

"Do you mind if I ask you a personal question?"

"No," the Queen replied, "but I might not be able to give you a full answer."

"Do you like football?" Tommy asked.

"Well, not really," the Queen answered.

"In that case," said Cooper, "do you mind if I have your Cup Final tickets?"

The Queen is apparently a big fan of the BBC's satirical TV show, *Have I Got News for You*. One evening, the British actor Brian Blessed used the f-word during the programme before describing in great detail how climbers manage to go to the toilet on Mount Everest.

Shortly afterwards, the Queen met him, and said, "That was a funny story you told about going to the toilet on Everest, Mr Blessed." It seems that she also wanted to put his mind at rest about swearing on TV, and told him: "Fuck is an Anglo-Saxon word."

Tracy Emin is a notorious English artist, famous for shocking the establishment with works like "My Bed" (which was literally her unmade, and none too hygienic-looking, bed). In 2011, the Queen went to the opening of an exhibition in Kent, and was introduced to Emin. She deflated the artist's ego by asking: "Do you show internationally as well as in Margate?"

When the star American photographer Annie Leibovitz was commissioned to take an official portrait of the Queen in 2007, she was firmly put in her place. The American asked the Queen to take off her crown to make the image "less dressy". The Queen retorted: "Less dressy? What do you think this is?"

In 1966, the Queen looked delighted to shake hands with England captain Bobby Moore when she presented him with the World Cup – especially because the world's television viewers saw him wiping his hands on the tablecloth before meeting her, so that he wouldn't get the royal white gloves dirty. However, she seems less keen on modern footballers, and once asked the Premier League Chairman, Sir David Richards, "Aren't they prima donnas?"

When presenting an award to British film and TV director John Schlesinger in 1970, the Queen appears to have made a risqué reference to his gayness. Schlesinger had recently made the hit movies *Midnight Cowboy* and *Marathon Man*, and was awarded a CBE for his services to film. Later in life, the openly gay Schlesinger himself liked to tell the story of how the Queen gave him the award. Having trouble putting the medal ribbon over his head, she said, "Now, Mister Schlesinger, we must try and get this *straight*."

Schlesinger insisted that she then gave him a knowing look that proved she was deliberately making a gay pun.

5   THE ROYAL WARDROBE

The Queen is famous for her outfits. Or rather, infamous, because over the decades she has developed a style of her own which mainly involves wearing colours that no one else would dare to don. During her 90th birthday celebrations in 2016, for example, the Queen was pictured in a green so bright it looked as though it had been invented to scare off insects.

The reason for this garishness is well-known – the Queen must be the most visible person at any occasion. Wherever she is, she is the star, and when there is no jewelled tiara or crown on her head to focus onlookers' attention, she needs colour. The Queen herself explained it perfectly: "If I wore beige, nobody would know who I am."

As she has got older, her outfits have grown more colourful, perhaps to compensate for her whitening hair and paling complexion. In 2012, Stewart Parvin, who has been one of the royal stylists since 2000, suggested another reason for the brightness. He explained in a newspaper interview that the Queen is "very tiny", and that he uses bright, monochromatic colours, as opposed to motifs, to "elongate" her.

Mr Parvin also gave away some of the Queen's other fashion secrets. He revealed, for example, the startling fact that one of her shoulders is higher than the other, so she needs an extra shoulder pad to compensate. Not very gallant of him.

Even more intimately, Mr Parvin praised the Queen for being a "cold person" – in the sense that she doesn't perspire. The lack of royal perspiration, he said, was the reason why the Queen's outfits never look creased. This news must have shocked quite a few older Brits, for whom imagining the Queen doing something as physical as sweating is akin to treason. (Incidentally, members of the Queen's staff have confirmed that she never perspires, but emphasize that it's not an advantage – the human body uses sweat to cool down, so when the Queen is trussed up in heavy robes at an airless midsummer ceremony, she is in real danger of overheating.)

Mr Parvin also described how the Queen avoids blistered feet by having a servant wear in her shoes for her before she herself puts them on. This is an old trick – Napoleon used to do the same thing with his black hats. It's as if an uncomfortable shoe or hat rim might cause the downfall of a kingdom or empire.

Another royal insider, Angela Kelly, who makes many of the Queen's hats, disclosed that the monarch has small weights inserted in the hems of her garments, so that skirts and jackets don't blow up in the wind. Ms Kelly advised Kate Middleton, the Duchess of Cambridge, to do the same, though from the revealing photos of Kate we've all seen in the press, it doesn't look as though the advice was heeded.

Angela Kelly helps the Queen to choose the right colour for each occasion – "happy" tones for a school visit, for instance, or a colour that contrasts with green vegetation if she is going to a garden. She doesn't want to disappear on the lawn.

Another piece of inside information divulged by Ms Kelly was that royal sleeves are kept short for banquets, so that the Queen doesn't dunk her dress in the soup.

The most essential secret, though, has to be how the Queen ensures the surprise factor every time she arrives at a public ceremony. This is simple – a spread sheet is kept, recording when the Queen wore which outfit, or even which colour predominated. If she wears blue on a trip to Scotland, for example, it might be years until she wears it there again. The Queen wears most of her outfits more than once – she doesn't want to be seen as wasteful – but they are strictly rotated so that there is enough time for the public and the journalists to forget them.

A few more clothes-related anecdotes ...

In 1945, near the end of the Second World War, the future Queen served for three weeks in the Women's Auxiliary Territorial Service. This was of course largely a morale-boosting tactic for propaganda purposes, so Elizabeth was warned that she would be photographed in uniform. However, the image-conscious Princess didn't want to be seen in the ordinary baggy khaki uniform of the Women's Service. She therefore had her jacket taken in so that it would flatter her bust and waistline. This wasn't just a royal privilege, however – during the war, both male and female officers often had their trousers and jackets tailored to look more elegant than the notoriously ill-fitting standard-issue uniforms.

It was said in 1947 that the young Princess Elizabeth paid for her wedding dress with 300 clothing coupons. In post-war Britain rationing was still in force, and stocks of fabrics were severely limited. Generous members of the public therefore sent their own clothing coupons to Buckingham Palace, but the Princess returned them all because it was illegal to take other people's rations.

In any case, the story was only partly true. There probably weren't enough clothing coupons in the whole country to pay for a royal wedding dress embroidered with 10,000 pearls. In fact, the designer, Norman Hartnell, was paid £1,200 for the dress – at the time, roughly the cost of a three-bedroomed house in the London area.

The Queen's nursemaid when she was a baby was Margaret MacDonald, known to the family as "Bobo". Ever afterwards, Bobo always had something to say about the Queen's outfits. She was the only person allowed to tell the Queen directly "you look awful in that". Bobo was not a fan of the designer Hardy Amies, who became one of the Queen's dressmakers just before she acceded to the throne. As the Queen was knighting Amies in 1989, she whispered to him: "Bobo will give me hell for this."

These days, when the Queen is having clothes fitted at one of her homes, she is careful to make sure than no pins or needles are left on the floor, for fear that one of her corgis might prick itself.

When on tour, the Queen packs three outfits per day for her various public appearances – as well as a set of black mourning clothes, in case someone important drops dead.

The Queen is said to consider royal regalia, including the crown and her most splendid ceremonial robes, as a sort of uniform rather than a sign of her own personal splendour. Her sister Margaret once summed up this point of view: "The Queen is the only person who can put on a tiara with one hand while walking downstairs."

When the Queen was getting ready to give her televised Christmas speech in 1990, she asked the director: "Clothes-wise, does it look all right with the background?" He said he was happy with the colour combination, to which the Queen replied that it was "jolly lucky, because it would be awful if you said no – I'd have to find something else."

The Queen is not allowed to intervene in party politics, but in 2017 she seems to have made her feelings about one political issue clear with the not-so-subtle use of her wardrobe. When opening parliament on 21 June 2017, she was obliged to read out the speech prepared for her by the government, announcing their plans to implement Brexit. As soon as the royal limousine arrived at the Houses of Parliament, the social media went into overdrive at the sight of the Queen's hat – it was European blue, and crowned with yellow-centred flowers. In short, a 3D version of the EU flag.

Amongst the many commentators was one of the European Parliament's negotiators on Brexit, Belgian MEP Guy Verhofstadt, who tweeted "Clearly the EU still inspires some in the UK".

Buckingham Palace later refused to comment on the hat, but many have interpreted it as an example of the Queen's humour – combined with her acute sense of diplomacy. After all, if you're reading out a speech announcing separation from your European neighbours, it's only polite to compensate by wearing their colours.

Royal Accessories

The Queen is famous for her ever-present handbags. There is much speculation about what they might contain. According to royal insiders, the contents usually include very practical items such as lipstick and a mirror, for quick top-ups. The Queen is said never to carry cash, but she has been known to put money into the collection plate in church – she seems to think that every person has to pay their own debt to the deity.

Whenever the Queen is going to a sit-down function of any kind, her handbag usually contains a hook so that she can hang the bag from the table rather than putting it on the floor. It's hard to believe anyone would try to steal the Queen's handbag, so she probably just wants to avoid servants accidentally kicking it – or corgis doing something even worse.

When the Queen takes the handbag off the hook and places it on the table, it is a sign to her staff (and everyone else) that she is ready to leave. She only puts her bag on the floor if she is terribly bored and is begging a member of her staff to get her out of there immediately. When standing up, at a garden party for example, if she is tired of talking to someone, she moves her handbag from arm to arm so that someone will come and rescue her.

However, given that these "secret" handbag codes have been publicized in the press and become common knowledge, the Queen may well have invented a new system to avoid insulting people. It would be interesting to observe her at a function and watch out for any unusual handbag gestures, such as waving it above her head to attract an aide's attention, or dropping it on a boring person's foot.

When former James Bond actor Roger Moore was invited to Buckingham Palace, his wife accompanied him, and she asked the Queen why she carried her handbag around indoors. The Queen replied: "This house is very big, you know."

It is said that Margaret Thatcher admired the Queen's habit of carrying a handbag during official visits – it was a clear sign that she is a woman, and a hint that she is a normal person with a need to carry normal things around. Mrs T therefore adopted the handbag as a symbol of her supposed down-to-earth political values. Though her male ministers were more afraid that she would use it as a weapon.

Like her outfits in general, the Queen's choice of umbrellas reflects her desire to let the public see her. She often carries a transparent umbrella so that no one's view of her will be blocked, and she has a collection of about a dozen, with coloured rims and handles so that they can match her outfit.

The Queen's habit of carrying her own umbrella amused onlookers in June 2014, when she visited Paris and went on a walkabout in the unseasonal rain with the city's mayor, Anne Hidalgo. While the Queen carried her own transparent umbrella (rimmed in black to match her shoes and handbag), Ms Hidalgo was accompanied by a male underling, who was carrying an umbrella to protect her from the downpour. But then, France's politicians often consider themselves to be more royal than the royals.

6   INSIDE THE ROYAL HOMES

The Queen has as many homes as you would expect of someone who comes from a family that has never had to sell anything to pay inheritance tax. The houses tend to be on the large side, too, so it's lucky she doesn't have to mow the lawn or mop the floors herself. Buckingham Palace, for instance, has 240 bedrooms and 78 bathrooms.

Some of these houses belong to the Queen personally, while others are official residences that she occupies as a monarch rather than a homeowner.

First and foremost, there is Buckingham Palace, the royal London residence, especially during the week. Windsor Castle, about 35 kilometres southwest of London, is the Queen's main country residence, where she spends most weekends, as well as longer periods during Ascot racing season. Meanwhile, Holyroodhouse in Edinburgh is the castle where the Queen stays when on official business in Scotland.

These three houses do not belong to the Queen – they are owned by the Crown Estate, a public body founded in 1961 to manage land and buildings that used to be owned or administered by the monarchy. Today, rents and various profits from the properties (which include 100,000 hectares of forest, salmon fishing rights in Scotland, Ascot racecourse, and half of Britain's shoreline) go to the nation.

The Queen has two personally-owned homes. Sandringham, a house with 8,000 hectares in Norfolk, was bought in 1862 by Queen Victoria as a home for her son, the future King Edward VII, ironically because wanted a place to escape the attentions of his disapproving mother. The Queen spends Christmas and January there.

Balmoral Castle, with its 20,000 hectares of woodland, grazing land, mountains and grouse moors, was acquired by Victoria's husband, Prince Albert, in 1852. The estate also houses a whisky distillery that produces 400,000 litres of alcohol per year – not all of it for the Queen's personal consumption, of course.

The Queen shares some of her homes with the general public. Any tourist can buy a ticket and nose around Buckingham Palace, Windsor Castle or Sandringham to admire the superb royal art collections, the lavish decorations, and the well-tended gardens. But of course you won't get to see the Queen wandering about in her dressing gown or putting her feet up to watch TV.

The royal apartments are quite naturally off limits, and the only real glimpses we get of the Queen's everyday life are the ones that the royal publicity machine gives us – or when former staff spill the beans.

Staff indiscretions happen very rarely, because the Queen's attendants tend to be loyal people who respect their boss's request for privacy. Not only that, they sign a confidentiality agreement. And anyone who flouts the contract incurs royal displeasure at their peril. The earliest example of this came in 1950 when a retired nanny called Marion Crawford (known by the royal household as "Crawfie") published a book about her experiences bringing up Princesses Elizabeth and Margaret. *Little Princesses* was a sugary, affectionate account of life at the palace, but when the book came out, Crawfie was forced to leave the home she had been given on retirement, and was deleted from the royal Christmas card list for life. Merciless punishment.

Some of the most intimate details of the Queen's home life, such as the fact that she helps herself to breakfast muesli from a Tupperware box, have come from an undercover reporter called Ryan Parry, who spent two months in 2003 working as one of the Queen's footmen, and then wrote up his revelations for a newspaper. It was an almost treasonable betrayal of the monarch's trust – but he did reveal some fascinating stuff ...

According to Parry, the Queen hates the sound of ice cubes clinking in drinks. Her homes therefore have ice makers that produce "spherical cubes" of ice, which apparently make less noise in the glass.

Similarly, the Queen likes sandwiches to be cut into octagons – apparently she is superstitious, and thinks that rectangular sandwiches are too like coffins. (Though it takes quite a stretch of the imagination to imagine a coffin full of cucumber slices.)

When she is at home, the Queen writes requests for meals in a menu book. She also uses it to leave notes for staff. She once left a live slug next to the book, with a note: "I found this in the salad. Could you eat it?"

More insights into royal home life

When not at a formal banquet, the Queen is fond of simple cooking. She is said to hate gastronomic fussiness. On one occasion, when she was served salmon and scrambled eggs, with a whole lemon on the plate, she sent the lemon back to the kitchen with a note: "This is a waste".

The Queen loves the peace and quiet of Balmoral, her Scottish castle. She appreciates it all the more because her London homes are in the thick of urban noise. Buckingham Palace is next to a roundabout, and Windsor Castle is right in Heathrow Airport's flight path. Once, during a lunch at Windsor, the Queen astonished guests by announcing "747 … Airbus" as different planes flew over. She was able to identify the planes from the sound they made.

People who are invited to small, informal meetings with the Queen are often amazed to see her acting just like a normal hostess. Once, when receiving some Canadian diplomats at Windsor, she gave them a snack lunch. One of the Canadians later admitted that he couldn't believe it when the Queen told a male guest: "You sit there and be Daddy. I'll sit here and be Mummy."

Guests at Balmoral have sometimes heard the Queen telling a story about a dinner there, when grace was said by a local clergyman who made an inadvertent double entendre. The Queen was so amused that she made him part of her repertoire of impressions, and apparently mimics the Scottish accent perfectly as she repeats his prayer: "For the delicious meal we are about to receive, *and for the intercourse afterwards*, may the Lord make us truly thankful."

Every year in June, the Queen invites the 24 members of the Order of the Garter to lunch at Windsor Castle, followed by a church service in the chapel. The so-called Garter Day sounds very sexy but is in fact a procession of a couple of dozen rather aged men and women (membership is for life) trooping through the castle grounds in blue velvet robes and enormous black feathered caps. On hot days, the Queen (who also wears the robes) and her ancient knights and dames bake, and on one occasion the 95-year-old former Prime Minister James Callaghan tripped over his robe and ended up on his backside. The Queen sympathized with him: "Whoever invented these robes wasn't very practical, even in the days when somebody wore clothes like these." (The order was created in 1348.) These days, the Queen makes the occasion as comfortable as possible. She, Prince Philip and the members of the order walk down to the chapel and then ride in carriages and cars back up to the castle. The Queen put it plainly: "It's always very lucky to plod downhill and not uphill."

Strictly speaking, the Queen has exclusive hunting rights on the land surrounding her country homes. But she doesn't seem to be an over-possessive landlady. Once, while driving around Balmoral, she spotted two men carrying shotguns and full game bags. They'd been poaching. The Queen burst out laughing and said, "There's nothing like catching the Chief Superintendent poaching."

It's so hard to get good servants nowadays ...

The Queen's household consists of about 1,200 people, from the Lord Chamberlain, at the head of the Royal Household, right down to cleaners, dishwashers and the people who muck out her horses.

Today the Queen's employees include modern professionals in IT, security and marketing, but there are also some wonderful old job titles such as the Astronomer Royal, the Queen's Bargemaster, a Surgeon Gynecologist to the Queen (not a post required for kings, of course), the Keeper of the Jewel House, and the Queen's Piper, whose main job is to play the bagpipes underneath the Queen's window at 9am every day for 15 minutes – not every guest's favourite alarm call.

For workaday jobs in the royal household, there are regular adverts on the royal website:

theroyalhousehold.tal.net

At the time of writing there was an opening for an apprentice bookbinder at Windsor Castle. Perhaps the Queen wants to preserve her horse-racing magazines for posterity.

Staff who will be in regular contact with the monarch get rigorous training before being allowed into the royal presence. Even so, their first times serving the Queen can be nerve-racking. One victim of first-night nerves almost got himself fired during a meal at Christmas 2004. Seeing the Queen stand up, he thought she was leaving the table, and promptly pulled her chair out of the way, as he had been trained to do. Unfortunately, the Queen changed her mind, and went to sit down again, ending up on the floor. There was a shocked silence – before the Queen herself laughed.

The Royal yacht *Britannia,* which was decommissioned in 1997, was a haven where the Queen went to relax at the end of her summer duties. The crew were therefore recruited according to even stricter criteria than her usual staff. At job interviews, they were asked just two questions: whether they had a criminal record, and if they possessed a sense of humour. A recruiting officer explained: "If they laughed at the first [question], there wasn't any need for the second."

Once, while the Queen was out on a pheasant shoot, a wounded bird flew out from behind a hedge and knocked her over. She was spattered with its blood, and her bodyguard thought she had been shot. He instantly dived to the ground beside her and began to perform mouth-to-mouth resuscitation.

Describing the incident later during sittings with the painter Lucian Freud, the Queen told the artist: "The detective assumed I'd been shot and dived on top of me ... We got to know each other rather well."

However, she didn't disapprove of this physical contact at all. On the contrary, she was so impressed by the bodyguard's prompt action that she made him a member of her regular security detail.

On 13 June 1981, the Queen was riding her horse up the Mall during her birthday parade – side-saddle, as usual, without head protection – when a 17-year-old unemployed Englishman called Marcus Serjeant fired six shots at her from a handgun. Fortunately the bullets were blanks, but her shocked horse jerked forwards, almost throwing the Queen off. She calmed the horse and the parade carried on, but her security staff decided that during future parades she would be flanked on either side by an army cavalryman. When one of the first riders took his place, the Queen teased him: "You know why you're here. You're the one to get shot, not me."

According to a report in the *Times* newspaper, a few years ago the Queen was almost shot by one of her guards. Apparently, whenever she suffers from insomnia, the monarch goes for a walk in the gardens of Buckingham Palace. She was doing this one dark night at 3am when an armed security guard saw a figure moving about in the shadows.

"Who's that?" he shouted, getting ready to repel an intruder.

Before he could fire a warning shot, a familiar face emerged into the light.

"Bloody hell, your Majesty, I nearly shot you," he told the Queen, before swiftly apologizing for his bad language.

Apparently unflustered by her brush with death, the Queen replied,

"That's quite all right. Next time I'll ring through beforehand, so you don't have to shoot me."

The Queen showed far more regal composure than her son Prince Andrew. When he was challenged by Buckingham Palace guards in September 2013, he flew into a rage. He was taking a stroll in the gardens in broad daylight when two armed security guards drew their guns and ordered him to "verify his identity".

Andrew apparently growled "don't you know who I am?", turned bright red in the face and, according to a "royal source" quoted in the press, became "incredibly, incredibly angry" and "shouted at them like a schoolteacher".

The police officers later made a personal apology, and a few days later Prince Andrew issued a statement saying, "I am grateful for their apology, and look forward to a safe walk in the garden in the future."

He obviously didn't take a lesson from his calm mother.

In July 1982, an intruder called Michael Fagan avoided security and got an unauthorized insight into the Queen's private life. He broke into Buckingham Palace, and the Queen woke up in the night to find Fagan standing by her bed – barefoot, wearing a Tshirt and jeans, and nursing a bleeding hand that he had cut while breaking a window. The Queen kept him talking, and then managed to get away by offering to go and fetch him a cigarette. She quickly found a chambermaid who alerted security.

Afterwards, the Queen told her family about her adventure, giving a perfect imitation of the shocked chambermaid's Yorkshire accent: "Bloody 'ell, Ma'am, what's 'e doin' 'ere?"

Although the Queen has often been flippant about her own safety, she looks out for her staff. In 1982, Ronald and Nancy Reagan visited Britain and were given a state banquet at Windsor Castle. Afterwards, the Queen and Ronald Reagan paraded out of the banqueting hall along the aisle between the tables and two rows of chairs that had been pushed back so that the diners could stand up. This procession was preceded by the Lord Chamberlain, a 66-year-old Scotsman called Charles Maclean, who, as protocol dictated, had to walk backwards, facing the Queen. Mr Reagan noticed that she was giving him hand signals – left a bit, right a bit – and she explained: "We don't get those chairs even, and he could fall over one and hurt himself."

The staff at the various royal residences know that the Queen keeps a keen eye on them. Once, at Windsor Castle, she asked an army officer, "Do the Welsh Guards have new uniform requirements? Are red socks allowed?" Apparently she had noticed a guardsman in the grounds that day wearing red socks instead of the uniform green.

Trusted staff can enjoy very long careers in the Queen's service. Her nursemaid and dresser Margaret "Bobo" MacDonald first looked after the Queen as a baby and stayed in her entourage for 67 years, looking after her clothes and jewels and acting as a confidante. In 1967, while accompanying the Queen on a visit to a stud farm in Normandy, Bobo wandered away, only to be arrested by French gendarmes as a potential stalker, much to the Queen's amusement. When Bobo died in 1993, aged 89, she was still living in an apartment in Buckingham Palace.

The Queen's press secretary Martin Charteris served the Queen for 27 years, from 1950-77. When he retired, the Queen told him "Martin, thank you for a lifetime" and gave him a silver tray.

Martin was crying (unlike the Queen), but managed to quip: "The next time you see this, it will have a gin and tonic on it."

The Queen enjoys teasing her domestic staff. Once, after going out shooting at the Sandringham estate in Norfolk, she couldn't get out of her tight, muddy waterproof leggings. She summoned a footman and made a very un-royal request: "Would you pull my pants off?"

7 AN ALMOST NORMAL QUEEN

The Queen can't behave entirely like other people. She has to demand, and show, respect for her status as head of the institution of constitutional monarchy.

Even her birthdays aren't normal. Unlike everyone else, she has two – one on the anniversary of her birth (21 April), the other in June. The second is an official birthday, a tradition started by King George II. His actual birthday was in November, and he was afraid that the weather would be too bad for his celebrations, so he decided to hold an official commemoration in summer, and the Queen has preserved the tradition. She, however, made one change – the monarch's official birthday is now at the weekend (on the second Saturday in June) so that the public can attend without having to take a day off work. A nice human thought.

The only real denial of the Queen's human status is the ban on any media mention of Her Majesty going to the toilet. No report, no documentary – or none in Britain, anyway – ever mentions this. The royal bodily functions are taboo. All we know, through whispered rumours, is that when the Queen visits a building, there must be a toilet available for her *exclusive* use. On that day, no non-royal buttocks must touch that seat.

In other ways, though, the Queen delights the public with her sudden displays of humanity – most of all, her jokes making fun of herself. Let's face it, none of these jokes are really as hilarious as the media try to pretend, but if everyone is so impressed whenever she makes a self-deprecating quip, it is because of this dichotomy between her two identities, as a ceremonial figurehead and an ordinary lady who enjoys a laugh at her own expense. It's as if a royal portrait in the National Gallery suddenly winked at us, or a statue of Napoleon farted. We're laughing in surprise at this sudden human touch. Here are a few examples ...

While watching television highlights from the 1981 wedding of Prince Charles and Princess Diana, the Queen apparently exclaimed, "Oh, look! I've got my Miss Piggy face on!", referring of course to the coquettish pig puppet in *The Muppets*. The name instantly became an inside joke in the royal household, and for her 60th birthday in 1986, Buckingham Palace staff members gave the Queen a birthday card depicting Miss Piggy in royal regalia. When she saw the card, the Queen apparently "burst into peals of laughter."

(Even so, this doesn't mean that it would ever be wise to tell the Queen she looks like a pig.)

The Queen says that she doesn't want to be accompanied by flashing lights and police sirens when she is driven through the streets, because, she explained, "I'd be like Idi Amin or Gaddafi."

One evening, when the Queen was on her way to a private party in London – therefore probably in a Range Rover rather than a royal limousine – her vehicle was stopped by a procession of cars with a police escort. The Queen commented: "It must have been a very important ruler."

At a dinner to mark D-Day, the Queen was seated between two members of different European royal families, while Presidents Clinton and Mitterrand were sitting much further away along the table. Advisors suggested that royal protocol might be relaxed, so that the Queen could sit between the two politicians. She agreed instantly. "After all," she said, "I can see my cousins any time I like."

When the Dean of Windsor went to tell the Queen that he was going to retire, she replied: "That's all right for you. I can't."

Often, though, she is able to take a more detached view of her role. Although she is said to have suffered over Princess Diana's apparent desire to become the most famous person in the royal family, the Queen managed to joke about the situation. In the 1990s, while both the Queen Mother and Diana were alive, she asked a member of her staff: "My mother's a star. My daughter-in-law's a star. Where does that leave me?"

In 1961, there was a press scandal over reports that the royal yacht *Britannia* was being refitted at a cost of

£2 million. This was an unthinkable amount – at the time the average annual salary in Britain was under £1,000.

The Queen hadn't been told about the refit, and summoned First Lord of the Admiralty to ask who was paying. He said that as it was a state-owned ship, it was the Admiralty (part of the Ministry of Defence). The Queen replied: "I see. You pay and I get the blame."

The Queen is famous for her joy when one of her horses wins a race. That could genuinely count as a personal triumph, because as the owner, she receives the prize money. But she apparently spreads this sense of personal victory more widely. On one occasion, when England won a cricket match, she was heard by her staff to shout, "I've won!"

In November 2015, five months before her 90th birthday, the Queen attended the Commonwealth Heads of Government Meeting in Malta, at which the Canadian Prime Minister Justin Trudeau gave a speech praising the Queen for her "long and tireless service." She began her reply by quipping, "Thank you, Mr. Prime Minister of Canada, for making me feel so old."

In June 2016, a few days after Britain voted to leave the EU, the Queen went to Northern Ireland, where she met Deputy Minister Martin McGuinness. He asked her how she was, and she gave an answer that anyone her age might come out with: "Well, I'm alive, anyway."

Personal Tastes

In 2006 the English writer Alan Bennett published a witty novella, *The Uncommon Reader*, in which he imagined the revolution in royal life that would be caused if the Queen suddenly became a passionate fan of literature – she might interrupt her meetings with the Prime Minister to discuss Jane Austen, organize parties for writers rather than bishops and diplomats, or ask members of the public what they think of certain books instead of just saying, "thank you, what lovely flowers."

Bennett's story was a joke about the need for the monarch to perform her duties as her royal function requires, and not suddenly become a fanatic about something that distracts her from her official role. In fact, of course, the Queen does have personal tastes in literature and other forms of culture, and thanks to newspaper reports and royal leaks, we know a little about them …

The Queen has never enjoyed intellectually-challenging literature – during the reign of her grandfather George V, the poet TS Eliot came to give a private reading of his best-known, but notoriously difficult, work, *The Wasteland*. His obscure language and monotonous voice did not go down very well, and the Queen Mother later reported that: "the girls [Elizabeth and Margaret] got the giggles".

As far as her own reading is concerned, the Queen's tastes are said to be relatively simple. As one of her entourage revealed: "If it isn't to do with horses or racing, she's not interested." Two of her favourite authors are Dick Francis and Jilly Cooper, both of whose books are very horsey. Francis was a former racing jockey who wrote novels set in the world of horse racing. Jilly Cooper is perhaps a more surprising choice for an elderly Queen – her books are often racy, and the cover of her novel *Riders* features a gloved hand resting on the buttock of the tightest riding breeches in the history of literature, with a whip hovering provocatively nearby. Then again, with Prince Harry in the family, there is probably nothing that shocks the Queen.

Denys Rhodes, the husband of the Queen's cousin Margaret Rhodes, was a writer, and the Queen was at a party when she overheard him announcing that he had finished writing a new thriller. "I just need a title," he told everyone. The Queen chipped in: "I can't think of a reason for giving you one." It is, so far, her only known publishing-related pun.

The Queen's taste in music is as risqué as her favourite novels. She has said that, like many people of her generation, she loves the music of English singer George Formby, who was most famous in the 1930s and 1940s: "I know all his songs and I can sing them," the Queen has said.

Two of Formby's most famous songs were "When I'm Cleaning Windows", which is about what a man might see when peeping into people's bedrooms, and "With My Little Ukelele in My Hand", a double entendre song about his penis. It would be fun to hear the Queen sing that one.

The Queen is not a big fan of "modern" pop music. When she heard the close harmonies of the Everly Brothers singing their big hit of 1960, "Cathy's Clown", the Queen told a lady-in-waiting: "They sound like two cats being strangled".

Prince Philip has been equally scathing about music. In 2001, listening to Elton John at the Royal Variety Performance, Philip was heard to growl: "I wish he'd turn the microphone off!" And in 2002, he wanted to be prepared for a similar experience, so when told that he was going to hear Madonna sing her James Bond theme song at the premiere of *Die Another Day*, Philip asked: "Are we going to need earplugs?"

The Queen has a magnificent art collection that includes priceless works by Leonardo Da Vinci, Rembrandt, Rubens, and every great British painter since medieval times. Altogether, the Royal Collection includes 7,000 oil paintings, 30,000 watercolours and drawings, and half a million prints. But of course the Queen didn't choose all of these. Most were acquired by her ancestors, or gifted to the family, and the collection is managed by curators, with the pictures belonging to the nation rather than the monarch herself.

We know that the Queen keeps abreast of trends in modern art. Once, when dining with an American jeweller, she told him: "I have heard that Damien Hirst has been using diamonds to make a jewelled skull, but I prefer the diamonds around my neck."

Her personal taste in art is best illustrated by the choice of paintings in her apartments. At Buckingham Palace, these are dominated by horses. However, she doesn't want to look at just any old horses …

In 2015 the German President Joachim Gauck presented the Queen with a portrait of herself as a child, on horseback. Painted by a neo-expressionist German artist, Nicole Leidenfrost, it showed a very pink Princess Elizabeth sitting on a horse that was mainly blue, with yellow, green and red splashes on its flanks. The Queen's reaction was abrupt: "That's a funny colour for a horse". One thing we know for sure: she is clearly not a neo-expressionist.

8   A MODERN MONARCH

A modern British monarch is the representative of a tradition dating back centuries, at the very least to 1603, when the English and Scottish monarchies were combined, or to 1660, when the British monarchy took on its current status and became subject to parliament.

At times during Queen Elizabeth II's reign, she and the royal family as a whole have been criticized for being aloof, cut off from the people in their inherited castles, as if they were over-conscious of their historic importance.

This was felt especially strongly when they paid no income tax – constitutionally they don't really have to, though they have only been truly exempt from income tax since the reign of George V in the early 20th century. Before that, Victoria and Edward VII paid taxes on their private earnings, which came largely from land rents. In 1993, the Queen decided that being free of taxes was bad for the royal image, so since then the family has made "voluntary payments" and its members have become much more open about their finances. In purely private wealth, it is estimated that the Queen is now about the 300th-richest person in Britain with a personal fortune of around £350 million – hardly enough to buy a new apartment in London these days.

This show of financial solidarity with ordinary citizens helped to improve the royal family's image, and make them feel more modern and in touch. But any benefit from this was cancelled out brutally four years later, after the death of Princess Diana on 31 August 1997.

It must be rare for the grandmother of a woman killed in a car accident to be declared public-enemy number one when she wasn't driving the car and hadn't sabotaged the brakes, but that is what happened to the Queen after Diana and her boyfriend Dodi Fayed ended their lives in a road tunnel in Paris on that late-summer night.

The Queen's reaction – or apparent lack of it – to Diana's death, when everyone else in Britain was bursting into tears at the loss of "the people's princess", was pretty well the severest test that the British monarchy has suffered since King Charles I's head was violently removed by a parliamentarian axeman in 1649. Rarely has republicanism risen so high in the British consciousness as in 1997, when, urged on by the sensationalist media, people accused the Queen of being heartless and out of touch with her subjects' sentiments.

It was the deepest low point in the Queen's reign, but her reaction to this criticism saved the situation, and is the reason why the monarchy is again so popular in Britain today.

Let's look in detail at the crisis and how the Queen handled it ...

How Princess Diana almost killed the monarchy

In 1978, when Prince Charles reached his thirtieth birthday without getting married, the royal family started to get nervous. After all, an heir to the throne has one job – to produce more heirs. Edward VII (heir to Victoria) married at 21 and had his first child when he was 22; Edward's heir George V had two sons by the time he was 30; and King George VI produced the future Elizabeth II just before he hit 31.

Charles, then, was a late developer. Worse, it was semi-public knowledge that he was having an on-off affair with a married woman, Camilla Parker-Bowles, to whom he had almost got engaged in the early 1970s. The royal family knew that this relationship had to be ended, and a new marriage candidate found – not necessarily a princess, but someone with impeccable aristocratic credentials.

Probably because Charles's heart wasn't really in it, they began looking around as if trying to choose a new car. The most important thing was practicality. And one day in 1980, Charles remembered a rather attractive Land Rover he had seen, a stylish model called Diana Spencer. To pursue the car metaphor – which is unashamedly tacky, but then the whole bride selection process seems to have been cynical in the extreme – this all-English car was a healthy pink colour, in excellent condition, possessed nice upholstery, and had (so everyone said) never been driven before. And if the metaphor seems to have gone way too far there, subsequent events will show that reality was even worse.

Diana Spencer came from an ancient British noble family descended from the Scottish royal house, the Stuarts (albeit via an illegitimate birth) and from the great British 17th-century general the Duke of Marlborough, an ancestor of Winston Churchill. Diana therefore had good blood – so good, in fact, that Charles had gone out with, and thought of marrying, Diana's elder sister, Sarah.

The only problem with this was that the Spencers were apparently so snobbish that they referred to the royals as "a German family" because of their Hanoverian origins and Queen Victoria's marriage to Albert of Saxe-Coburg. The Spencers were of "pure" British stock.

Charles had first met Diana in 1977, when she was only 16 and he was going out with Sarah. That was all – she was the little sister. Then in 1980, after Sarah got married, it apparently occurred to Charles that Spencer Mark 2 might be a good replacement. Diana was English, noble, 19, no doubt fertile. Ideal.

One of the most attractive things about Diana was that she was a virgin – so no chance that the tabloids would be able to rake up any muck about old boyfriends. And in a medieval-like ordeal, Diana had to submit to the humiliation of having a medical virginity test. Unfortunately for the Queen's image, it was commonly said at the time that she had insisted on the need for a bride without a murky past.

Charles told friends about Diana: "I don't love her,

but she has the best qualities," and he proposed marriage in February 1981.

The wedding took place just five months later on 29 July, and was watched on TV by an estimated 750 million around the world – so no pressure at all on the now 20-year-old girl marrying a man ten years older who was still "close" to his old flame Camilla.

Diana, who had become bulimic because of the public attention, press harassment and royal expectation, played her part in the fairy-tale TV wedding, and even followed through by delivering an heir, William, almost exactly nine months later. The perfect princess.

Or was she? During the honeymoon, part of which the poor girl had to spend with her parents-in-law at Balmoral, Diana was moody and withdrawn. Prince Philip later told a biographer: "She didn't appear for breakfast. At lunch she sat with her headphones on, listening to music." More like a temperamental teenager than the future of the British monarchy.

Back in London, Diana was being tracked night and day by the paparazzi, and the Queen took the unusual step of intervening with the press to protect her. She convened a meeting of Fleet Street editors to plead for leniency, telling them that Diana was afraid to leave her home at Kensington Palace – she couldn't even nip out to buy some sweets. Barry Askew, editor of the sensationalist *News of the World*, asked why Diana had to go out herself – why couldn't she send a servant to buy them? The Queen retorted: "That's the most pompous thing I've ever heard."

Diana produced yet another son, Harry, in 1984, so her dynastic duty was done, but the marriage was already shaky. Diana was so suspicious of Charles and Camilla that she became obsessed about any woman he was close to: according to one biographer, Diana even resented Charles's friendship with Nancy Reagan, the 63-year-old wife of President Ronald Reagan.

Diana also started to have flings, first with a bodyguard then her riding instructor. She also began to learn how to turn the endless press harassment to her advantage, harnessing it and using the media as they had used her. During a trip to India, she posed for photos alone in front of the Taj Mahal, looking as one newspaper put it, "wistful" and "solitary". She also contributed to a book that dished all the dirt on her marriage – and then steadfastly denied doing so when the media went into a frenzy, even after it was proved that she had helped the writer.

Worried about the future of his family, even crusty old Prince Philip stepped in and wrote long letters to Diana, offering advice about how to cope with marrying into the royal clan. Diana replied to him, apparently starting her letters "Dearest Pa" and ending them "with fondest love", but meanwhile she was telling friends that Philip had been sending her "wounding", "stinging" criticisms.

The writing was on the wall – or in envelopes at least – for a disaster that would wound and sting Charles, the Queen and the whole institution of the monarchy. It came in two stages.

First, inevitably, the marriage fell to pieces like a royal palace that has had a bomb planted in its foundations. Of course, it collapsed very publicly. A tabloid newspaper revealed a phone conversation between Diana and a lover, to whom she complained about being mistreated by the royals "after all I've done for this fucking family". She'd come a long way since the blushing virgin bride.

Then, apparently in revenge for a TV interview that Charles gave, in which he claimed to have been "faithful and honourable" to his wife, on 20 November 1995 (coincidentally – or not – the Queen and Prince Philip's 48th wedding anniversary), Diana staged the performance that has gone down in royal myth. With dark-shadowed eyes, gazing tragically into the camera, she told the nation the "truth" about her marriage – or her version of it. She came out with the memorable line: "There were three of us in this marriage, so it was a bit crowded." She was of course ignoring the fact that it had been made even more densely populated thanks to her own mob of lovers.

Diana also said that Charles probably wasn't up to the role of king: "I don't know whether he could adapt." And she even tried to usurp the Queen's role by saying that she wanted to be "a queen of people's hearts". That night, if the monarchy had been a democratic institution, Diana would have been elected its head, and the Queen would have been packed off to retirement at Balmoral, with all her corgis.

Predictably, Charles and Diana divorced in 1996, and the Queen was apparently relieved, thinking that the torment was over. She was wrong. Ever the media manipulator, Diana latched on to Tony Blair and became something of a poster girl for his election campaign, which led to him declaring her to be "the people's princess".

The Queen apparently took even this with a sense of humour – after he became prime minister in 1997,

Tony Blair gave colleagues a very credible impression of the Queen lecturing him: "Now, Blair, no more of this people's princess nonsense, I'm the people's Queen."

Although Diana was conducting fairly public love affairs, she was allowed to continue living in Kensington Palace, just across the park from Buckingham Palace, proving that the Queen was a pretty tolerant ex-mother-in-law. In summer 1997 Diana's choice of boyfriend was something of a challenge to the British establishment. He was Dodi Fayed, the son of the businessman Mohammed Al-Fayed, who owned Harrods, the famous London department store, as well as the Ritz Hotel in Paris.

Mr Al-Fayed, who was born in Egypt, had long been a thorn in the side of the establishment. In 1994, he had caused a government crisis by revealing that he had paid certain MPs to ask questions in parliament on his behalf. Later, he campaigned for Scottish independence from England, saying, "It's time for you to waken up and detach yourselves from the English and their terrible politicians ... When you Scots regain your freedom, I am ready to be your president."

Towards the end of August 1997 Diana travelled to Paris with Dodi to stay at the Ritz. She was still being mercilessly hassled by the paparazzi, and it was allegedly to try and shake off pursuers that the Ritz's head of security, Henri Paul, drove through the streets of the city at 200 kilometres per hour and smashed into a pillar near the pont de l'Alma at about 1am on Saturday 31 August, 1997.

The Queen was informed about the crash while she was staying at her Scottish home, Balmoral, and it was her immediate reaction that was to bring the monarchy close to its own demise.

Her press office issued a short, almost factual, statement: "The Queen and Prince of Wales [Charles] are deeply shocked and distressed by this terrible news." OK, there are two adjectives in there, but meanwhile the rest of Britain was suffering a public nervous breakdown. Flowers were being heaped outside Kensington Palace, and an endless stream of mourners came to gaze in silence at Diana's former home – silence, that is, except for the loud gushing of their tears.

Ever since that day in 1997, the British have thrown off their reputation for stiff upper lips and become the world's greatest weepers. No reality TV programme these days is complete unless the participants, both winners and losers, shed half their bodyweight in tears. Thanks to poor Diana, the nation that stoically lived through the Blitz now sobs with public emotion every time one of its citizens wins or loses a TV baking contest.

Back in August 1997, though, the Queen, failed to join in. She issued no further statements. When she went to church the next day, no prayer was said for Diana, even though William and Harry were in the congregation. She stayed in Scotland when the whole country seemed to be descending on Kensington Palace in London. The Queen refused to fly the flag at half-mast over Buckingham Palace – because tradition dictates that no flag at all flies there when she is away.

Meanwhile the Prime Minister Tony Blair was milking the media for attention. He made a speech declaring that he shared the pain of those who were mourning Diana, "the people's princess" – his obvious subtext being, unlike the heartless Queen.

The press cranked up the emotional atmosphere, splashing headlines across their front pages, like "WHERE IS OUR QUEEN?" and "SHOW US YOU CARE".

The conclusion in a growing number of people's minds was that the Sex Pistols were right – the Queen wasn't a human being.

This was, of course, nonsense. She had not gone on TV to weep, it was true. But then, neither had her parents after Buckingham Palace was bombed by the Nazis in 1940, almost killing them. And the Queen herself had hardly flinched, and had definitely not made a trembling public statement, after she had been shot at by a deranged gunman in 1981. The royal family had standards of imperturbability to uphold (or so she naively thought).

While the media, the people and Tony Blair flew into hysterics, the Queen had in fact been doing her best to shield and comfort William and Harry, and had refused to leave Scotland precisely because she wanted to keep the boys there in seclusion, away from the media attention that had contributed to their mother's death. And if she had dashed down to London to join the mourners, the press would have attacked her for abandoning her grandsons. She couldn't win.

In the end, though, public opinion (and especially the media's opinionating) became so hysterical that the Queen had to give in. She flew down to London, paid her respects at Diana's coffin, and even agreed to fly the Union Jack at half-mast over Buckingham Palace – the first time in history that it had ever been done. To resort yet again to a Second World War analogy, no one had demanded such a tribute to the fallen heroes of D-Day, let alone for a divorced princess who had died in a car accident. Things were getting out of hand.

The writer Alan Bennett summed up the oppressively populist mood perfectly when he said that the Queen was lucky not to have to do a TV phone-in. In fact, though, she had to do something pretty similar. For only the second time in her reign (the first was in 1991 after the Gulf War) she spoke live to camera outside of her annual Christmas message.

On 5 September 1997, the Queen delivered a stilted three-minute speech in front of a window at Buckingham Palace. Behind her, viewers could see the massed ranks of mourners. Dressed in black, looking decidedly uncomfortable, the Queen seemed to be thinking: "bloody Diana, bloody Blair, and bloody Charles – why couldn't he control her? I'll give him such a slap when I've finished this bloody speech" ... or something more queenly along those lines. She said that: "It is not easy to express the sense of loss" – and her own unease was clear for all to see. She added: "What I say to you now as a queen and a grandmother, I say from my heart," but looked much too calm and composed for this to be credible. Of Diana, she assured us: "I admired and respected her" – but the verb that everyone wanted to hear was "love". The Queen acknowledged that "thousands upon thousands of you expressed your grief most poignantly," but it sounded too artificial. In short, it would have been much more effective if she had just sat for three minutes and wept.

The most sincere part of the speech was when the

Queen said that: "I for one believe that there are lessons to be drawn from her life and from the extraordinary and moving reaction to her death" – because this was exactly what the Queen herself did to lift the monarchy out of the gloom and unpopularity of 1997.

The sovereign's public climb-down did not end the media disapproval. Allegations arose in the press that Diana had been assassinated on the orders of the royal family to stop her marrying a muslim, or having a muslim's baby – it was even alleged that Diana was pregnant at the time of the crash.

The rumours of a royal assassination took hold, and have never really gone away. I was in a small-town roadside café in Louisiana, USA, in 2006 when a man in a baseball cap, hearing my accent as I ordered breakfast, came over to my table. "You're English," he said, perceptively. "There's a question I've always wanted to ask an Englishman – did the royal family kill Diana?"

I realized that everyone in the café was looking over to my table, and felt obliged to stand up and give a short lecture on the subject, expressing my personal opinion that there would have been no sense in having Diana whacked – for a start, Diana's real importance to the royal family ended as soon as she produced two heirs to the throne. And anyway, her marrying a muslim would probably have been seen as a positive gesture of tolerance and national unity. Secondly, the royals would have known that if the story got out, which it inevitably would, then it would have meant the end of the monarchy, and there was no way they would have taken that risk.

I'm not sure the diners believed me – after all, in the southern states of the USA, not everyone believes in evolution, which seems like an obvious truth to me – but I personally thought my arguments were pretty convincing. However, the mere fact that I'd had to express them almost ten years after Diana's death was a sign of how far the public esteem for Britain's royal family had fallen, not just in Britain but all over the world.

It was the Queen, mainly with the help of William and Harry, who turned the situation around, by making the monarchy more open, more human, and yes, more humorous.

Is the Queen getting hip?

Ever since 1997, the Queen seems to have been on a mission to turn herself into the nation's cute grandmother. Obviously her Golden and Diamond Jubilees have helped, as have her 80th and 90th birthdays, her platinum (70th) wedding anniversary – and of course the wedding of Prince William and the speedy arrival of three royal babies, George, Charlotte, and Louis. Princess Kate, meanwhile, a sturdy middle-class girl, became the new people's princess, but one with a permanent smile. Prince Harry's marriage to Meghan Markle – an American TV star, a divorcee and – an historic first – one of African-American origin – will no doubt reinforce the image of one big happy royal family under the wing of the benevolent Queen. And with (at the time of writing) a red-headed African-American royal baby on the way, anything is possible.

William and Harry are perceived as almost-ordinary young men. They even speak with slangy accents when meeting the public, and have learnt how to use "like" in sentences where it is not needed, like anyone of their generation. (And incidentally, if any young reader is in doubt, the second "like" was necessary in that sentence.)

As the arrival of Meghan Markle has proved, everything about the monarchy has become more modern. Well, not *too* modern. Almost no one in Britain wants a Scandinavian-type system in which members of the royal family behave like ordinary citizens, where kings and queens ride around on bikes and make their own packed lunches. The Queen herself calls these "bicycle monarchies".

In general, most Brits today would confess that they enjoy the prestige of being the country that has the most flamboyant, ceremonial – and famous – monarchy in the world.

The Queen herself is at the heart of what has become a constant campaign to preserve the monarchy's popularity. She clearly realizes that modern touches make her seem more fun and more human. Though these have to be dosed, of course – she is not going to take a selfie while making a speech, or check her Facebook page during the State Opening of Parliament.

But since 1997, the signs that the Queen wants to be seen as a thoroughly modern monarch have been coming thick and fast ...

When meeting the Queen, men are supposed to bow, and women used to have to curtsey. Today, though, the Queen says that the curtsey is outdated: "not necessarily right for modern times".

In February 2003, the Queen went to a countess's 70th birthday party, which was being held in a London nightclub. Next day, on an official visit to St Alban's Abbey, just outside London, she met the Dean of the Abbey who asked her if she knew one of the other men attending the ceremony. "Oh yes," the Queen replied, "Robert and I were in a nightclub last night till half past one."

According to press reports, Prince Harry once bought the Queen a shower cap with the slogan: "Ain't life a bitch". Apparently she loved it. Sadly there are no photos of her wearing it (yet).

In 2001, during a visit to Oslo in Norway, the Queen attended the opening of an exhibition of paintings by the British painter Lucian Freud. The pictures included several of Freud's characteristically grotesque nudes, and the Queen was careful to stand well away from these, explaining that she didn't want to be "photographed between a pair of those great thighs".

In July 2014, during the Commonwealth Games in Glasgow, the Queen joined in one of the new rituals of modern life. As Australian hockey player Jayde Taylor was taking a selfie, the Queen, who was behind her, looked up and smiled into the camera. It was only when Jayde checked her shot that she discovered that she'd been photo-bombed by a smiling, green-hatted Queen.

In 2014, during a visit to London's Science Museum, the Queen sent her first-ever Tweet. It read: "It is a pleasure to open the Information Age exhibition today at the @ScienceMuseum and I hope people will enjoy visiting. Elizabeth R".

However, all she seemed to do was step up to a screen and hit the "Tweet" button. She didn't write the message herself.

In 2016, the royal family's press department published a photo of the Queen actually composing a Tweet – poking at a tablet with one finger. She was reacting to the congratulations she had received for her 90th birthday, and wrote: "I am most grateful for the many digital messages of goodwill I have received and would like to thank you all for your kindness. Elizabeth R."

It was a perfect 140 characters (Twitter's maximum back then) – the Queen proving that she was a natural Tweeter.

The Queen's most dramatic, and famous, piece of modernity has to be her appearance as an actress in the Opening Ceremony of the 2012 London Olympics, when she appeared alongside Daniel Craig in a miniature James Bond adventure filmed by the BBC.

Even Princes Charles, William and Harry knew nothing about the scheme, so they were as astonished as the millions of TV viewers around the world who watched the Queen meeting 007 at Buckingham Palace, then getting on board a helicopter and doing a fly-past of London's most famous monuments. The film ended as the helicopter was hovering over the Olympic Stadium, and the Queen apparently jumped out the door into the night sky.

The crowds in the stadiums and live TV viewers saw a real helicopter and a real figure in a pink dress parachuting down, before the Queen appeared in the stadium, walking towards her seat in the royal box to attend the ceremony. It was a perfectly executed royal joke, with the Queen at her deadpan best.

The skydiver was, of course a double who was dressed up in an exact copy of the peach-coloured dress that the Queen was due to wear that evening. His name was Gary Connery, though he was apparently no relation of former Bond actor Sean.

Everyone in Britain was amazed and delighted to see the Queen playing along with the joke. The press loved it, and the normally left-leaning *Daily Mirror* referred to "the Majesty of a movie star."

The Queen had apparently been in favour of the plan as soon as she heard about it. "It was not a case of having to persuade the Queen to take part," an official told a reporter. "Her Majesty said 'yes' to it straight away. She thought it was such brilliant fun. And when the idea for the format was explained to her she was happy with that, too. When we came to filming it, the Queen was a natural."

The director of the ceremony and the film segment, Danny Boyle, admitted that he originally planned for an actress to play the Queen, but was told: "Her Majesty would like to be in it herself." Apparently, the

Queen herself suggested her opening line: "Good evening, Mr Bond."

She even got roles for her corgis, who are seen escorting Bond into the royal apartments, sticking dangerously close to his vulnerable ankles, and then looking forlornly up as the helicopter takes off, as if they too were hoping to do some skydiving.

In any case, this was some of the best publicity that London, the Queen and the royal family as a whole have ever had. Only royal weddings and babies have outdone the Bond film – but the Queen is proving that the older generation can still do their bit.

The Queen was given another chance to make a movie in May 2016 when her grandson Prince Harry enlisted her to help publicize the Invictus Games, the sporting event for wounded military personnel. The film showed Barack and Michelle Obama indulging in some fighting talk ahead of the Games, to which the unimpressed Queen reacts by smiling indulgently, and saying, "Oh, really! Please!"

It was another fine performance from Britain's oldest comic actress. Prince Harry revealed that her scene was shot in just a few minutes: "She's the Queen, she's busy." He added that: "She's so incredibly skilled, she only needs one take." Harry was also sure that the Queen was relishing her new role as an on-screen comic actress: "You could see that look in her face, at the age of 90, thinking, 'Why the hell does nobody ask me to do these things more often?' "

Now there's an idea for a movie – Meghan Markle, Kate Middleton, Camilla and the Queen in *Prince Charlie's Angels* …

More Royal Revelations to Come?

Readers hungry for new nuggets of royal humour have only to follow Queen Elizabeth in the media. Journalists report her every public utterance, and the autobiographies of people who have met her are constantly hitting the bookshops.

But there may be an even more valuable, and as yet untapped, source of snippets – because the Queen keeps a diary, hand-writing her impressions about the day's events, and blotting them with black paper so no one knows what she's written.

She is on record as saying that her notes are not very detailed, and that writing the diary is just a daily habit "like scrubbing your teeth". But this suggests that her journal will consist of very personal, uncensored musings – and with any luck, these will include her spontaneous reactions to embarrassing situations or annoying people she has met, and maybe even a few jokes she has heard or told.

If the diary is ever released for public viewing, there could be a whole new series of royal quips to quote. However, that probably won't be any time in the near future. The personal diaries of Queen Victoria weren't published until 2012 – 111 years after her death. And there weren't any jokes in them.

Nevertheless, if Queen Elizabeth brings the same sense of fun to her diaries as she clearly does to her life, it might be worth the wait.

ABOUT THE AUTHOR

Stephen Clarke is a British author living in Paris, where he divides his time between writing and not writing.

He has written more than a dozen books. His best-known novels are the worldwide bestselling *Merde* series, including *A Year in the Merde* (which has sold more than one million copies worldwide) and *Merde Actually* (a number-one bestseller in the UK).

His non-fiction books include *1,000 Years of Annoying the French* (a number-one bestseller in the UK), a biography of King Edward VII's "education sentimentale" in France, called *Dirty Bertie, an English King Made in France*, as well as *Talk to the Snail: the Ten Commandments for Understanding the French*, and *How the French Won Waterloo (or Think They Did)*.

Clarke's book *1,000 Years of Annoying the French* inspired the permanent collection at a French museum, which he curated. It is the Centre Culturel de l'Entente Cordiale at the Château d'Hardelot in northern France.

He has written two stage shows – a cabaret-style adaptation of his novel *The Merde Factor*, and a words-and-music show in French called *L'Entente Cordiale en Paroles et Musique*. Both have been performed in France.

He also writes jokes for stand-up comedians and song words for singers, and has co-written a French radio sitcom and a radio play.

He occasionally performs in music and comedy clubs – but mainly for fun (his own rather than the audience's).

www.stephenclarkewriter.com   @sclarkewriter

Stephen Clarke

BY THE SAME AUTHOR

Fiction
A Year in the Merde

Merde Actually (published in the US as In the Merde for Love)

Merde Happens

Dial M for Merde

The Merde Factor

Merde in Europe

A Brief History of the Future

Who Killed Beano?

Non-Fiction
Talk to the Snail : the Ten Commandments for Understanding the French

Paris Revealed : the Secret Life of a City

1,000 Years of Annoying the French

Dirty Bertie, an English King Made in France

Château d'Hardelot, a Souvenir Guide

How the French Won Waterloo (or Think They Did)

The French Revolution & What Went Wrong

Printed in Great Britain
by Amazon

44041995R00088